ENGAGED COMMUNITY

the challenge of self-governance
in Waldorf education

ENGAGED COMMUNITY

the challenge of self-governance
in Waldorf education

Jon McAlice

Lindisfarne Books
2013

Lindisfarne Books
An imprint of SteinerBooks/Anthroposophic Press
610 Main Street, Great Barrington, MA 01230
www.steinerbooks.org

Library of Congress Cataloging-in-Publication Data
is available on request

Print ISBN: 978-1-58420-153-3
eBook ISBN: 978-1-58420-154-0

Contents

Introduction

For a number of years, my wife and I were at the center of a cooperative effort by homeschooling parents to provide a social and culturally supportive learning context for the children of the families involved. During this time, I was often asked what "my" school was called. My reply was that it wasn't a school, but was our contribution to the de-institutionalization of the American educational system. This book is similar. It is a contribution to the discussion concerning appropriate governance forms in Waldorf schools. It makes no pretense of being the final word on the subject. I leave that to others.

What I have focused on here is shifting the discussion around self-governance from a structurally-based approach to an ecological or dynamic approach. I have attempted to highlight and characterize the underlying concepts and practices that make such an approach possible. I hope that those who come to read this book will be able to discover in it a way of thinking about governance that will support them in developing their own approaches and help them find individual and unique solutions for their school or organization.

One of the primary obstacles on the path towards envisioning new approaches to self-governance lies in our thinking's inclination to grapple exclusively with what is, rather than what is in the process of becoming. We tend to focus more on the past than on the future. But the catastrophic ecological and social issues we now face do not allow us to continue to act in this way. We need to find another way to approach the problems we face and the challenges they present us. These offer us an opportunity to change not merely what we do now, but how we come to understand what tomorrow asks us to do. A friend of mine once pointed out that the future requires us to posit another form or dimension of existence, one that is just as real as what is, but only brings itself to expression in the form of potential. This is what comes to meet us every day in the laughter, the questions, and the anticipation of the learning child. It is the presence of the future in the present.

We tend to ignore this in many discussions concerning school governance, choosing to focus on tangibles rather than intangibles. But the intangibles are what make the difference.

The explorations that follow document my attempts to grapple with the intangibles. They have led me to ponder more deeply what I have come to recognize as the conditions of self-governance, the socio-cultural context that makes self-governance a sustainable reality. It has also become clear to me that the forms of governance a school adopts must grow and change as the school does. Just as a single approach cannot fit all schools, no one approach can meet the needs of a single school at all times.

I believe today that the healthiest way to approach the question of governance is to view self-governance as an ideal, something to strive for. It is for a community what the striving to achieve moral action born of freedom is for the individual. If the latter is not present, the former is unattainable. I feel I can say this with the same certainty and objectivity that I can say: This stone will remain where it lies until something comes along and moves it. Without individual striving, no true self-governance is possible.

Today, at a time when many of the long-practiced forms of self-governance in Waldorf education are falling by the wayside, it seems appropriate to contemplate why Rudolf Steiner placed such emphasis on the need for autonomous, teacher-led schools. At first glance, the answer is easy: to insure that children would be able to learn in an environment that is free of societal pressures. And who is in a better position to understand what children need than those who work with them each day, who have learned to recognize the signatures of their becoming, and whose knowledge is of the shared and practiced reality? Yet Steiner was adamant: for him, it isn't only a question of insuring that teachers can teach in freedom, but that their work should penetrate every aspect of the school. The school as a whole is to bear the signature of their shared striving.

Can children grow to freedom and social responsibility if they do not experience adults striving to do the same? No. The way teachers and parents work together to create and sustain a school is as much a part of the reality of Waldorf education as is what happens in the classroom. The quality of the adults' striving is reflected in the social culture of the student body. Adults must practice what they hope their children will live.

Waldorf schools are explicitly not anthroposophical schools. That said, it is also clear that no Waldorf school can thrive without a living interest in the approach to understanding human development out of which they grew. I have tried to keep the book as free of specifically anthroposophical vocabulary as possible in the hope that anyone who reads it will be able to come to an inner experience of the spiritual foundation upon which the content rests.

Throughout the book I have used the term colleagues in a descriptive rather than in a formal sense. It describes a quality of activity and relationship. A colleague is anyone in a school who is willing to engage in this quality of activity. Teachers, parents, administrative staff, groundskeepers, and Board members are all potential colleagues.

Finally, I have the pleasant task of expressing my gratitude to all those who over the years have contributed to the development of the ideas sketched out in the following pages. There have been too many to name each singly: colleagues in the schools where I have worked, parents in those schools, participants in workshops, late night conversations between friends. Special thanks go to Marisha Plotnik, Michelle Starr, and Beth Weisburn, who took the time to read through the manuscript and offer helpful suggestions. Heinz Zimmermann introduced me to many of the deeper riddles of the social dynamics of Waldorf schools. His work has been invaluable to me and I would like to express the deep gratitude with which I look back to the years we were able to work together.

Jon McAlice
Harlemville, New York, May 2013

1

The Challenge of Self-Governance

The question of governance has been at the center of an ongoing discussion in the Waldorf school movement for many years. As with many extended discussions, there have been times when the topic has been more in the forefront of colleagues' consciousness; at other times, when other issues have become more pressing, it has receded into the background. Today it has once again taken front stage. Sooner or later almost every conversation among colleagues or with parents circles around to various aspects of school governance. There have been moments of drama in the discussion, when someone, for instance, had the audacity to publicly question traditional approaches, or the translation of specific terms, or a school that had departed from officially sanctioned forms. The introduction of administrators by a small, then a growing number of North American schools has raised hackles among the old guard; and the recent advent of "administrative directors" with the increasing sense that teachers have enough to do in teaching without having at the same time to take responsibility for the institutional aspects of the school is one of the latest sore spots. The appointment of pedagogical "deans" is another. The discussion has at times been politically manipulated to insure that one model, the most widely accepted, the mainstream model, as it were, withstand any challenge raised against it.

Over the course of the last few years, conventional approaches to organizational development have become more and more prevalent throughout the movement. This is due no doubt in part to the increasingly complex legal environment and the burden of responsibility it places on the institution. It is easier to insure accountability in a clearly defined contractual context, within which the operative relationships are clearly objectified. The objectification of relationships can have a positive effect on institutional efficacy in the short-term; in the long-term, the depersonalization intrinsic to these organizational strategies inevitably leads to some form of passivity or to rebellion.

If one takes the time to read through the transcripts of Rudolf Steiner's meetings with the teachers of the first Waldorf school,[1] one discovers that the discussion concerning governance is in no way a recent phenomenon in Waldorf education. Questions concerning the relationship of the school to the Waldorf-Astoria factory were raised at the beginning of the second school year in 1920, and by the middle of the third year the point had been reached where dissension among the faculty made it necessary to appoint an executive council to manage the ongoing business of the school. For as long as Steiner remained involved—until shortly before his death in 1925—he functioned for all intents and purposes as the final authority in all school matters. In the above-mentioned transcripts, as well as in the lectures he gave for the teachers in those first years, we get a sense for how deeply Steiner was concerned about the social culture of the school. He seems to have had little patience for the intrigues and jockeying that began to arise. But he stepped back to let the teachers find a way to go forward themselves. The ideal of self-governance did not become a reality during those years, but a core group of teachers did take up the impulse to the full extent of their capabilities.

Today? We are still struggling. In fact, we are still struggling with many of the same issues that were being voiced then: trust in our colleagues' abilities, fear of our colleagues' gaining power, differences of opinion about what Waldorf really is, how to deal with perceived problems in a colleague's work, who is going to make which decision — very familiar issues. Have we not learned anything in the last ninety years? One would think that with so many schools all working on the same challenge, someone might have come up with a viable solution, an ideal form of governance for Waldorf schools. That is, however, not the case. We have no ideal forms. In fact, the forms many have held for ideal, perhaps even invested with quasi-divine authority, are proving ever less viable in practice. Many schools find themselves searching for something new, without really being clear about what they are looking for.

Perhaps the search for the ideal blinds us to some extent to the real question at hand. The challenge of self-governance is as much a part of our school movement as are the anthroposophical-anthropological explorations that laid its conceptual foundation. The striving to understand and give expression to the forces at work within the social context of a school is as much a part of what we offer children as a learning environment as what we do in the classroom. The struggle with self-governance and the pedagogical impulse in Waldorf education are inseparable. The Waldorf school is a proving ground for the conscious shaping of social interaction.

Consideration of the ongoing, sometimes exhausting challenge to develop and practice forms of self-governance that can enable us as a community to meet the needs of the children who come to us provides a positive starting point to look at this challenge more closely. Waldorf education becomes real when it is practiced. It can only prove itself in action. In Goethe's words: "What bears fruit, is true." This is also true about forms of self-governance. However we choose to approach it, the forms we adopt will have to prove their viability in practice.

Finding productive forms is easier if we have gained at least a partial understanding of what these forms need to achieve. What are our objectives, what do we hope to achieve through self-governance?

In speaking of education in general, Rudolf Steiner pointed out that a new focus was needed: "The real need of the present is that the schools be totally grounded in a free spiritual and cultural life. What should be taught and cultivated in these schools must be drawn solely from knowledge of the growing human being and of individual capacities. A genuine anthropology must form the basis of education and instruction. The question should not be: What does a human being need to know and be able to do for the social order that now exists? but rather: What capacities are latent in this human being, and what lies within that can be developed? Then it will be possible to bring ever-new forces into the social order from the rising generations. The life of the social order will be what is made of it by a succession of fully developed human beings who take their places in it. The rising generation should not be molded into what the existing social order chooses to make of it."[2] In order to achieve this shift in focus—a revolutionary shift with far reaching social implications—it was necessary to free teachers from the pressure placed on schools by business and governmental interests, and to place the development and implementation of curricula and teaching methods in their hands. School governance, teacher development, and decisions concerning educational practice would have to be carried by those who were directly involved in the students' learning, who through this involvement were direct participants in the learning process.

Education, in Steiner's view, was not a policy issue like waging war or developing international treaties, but a question of individual human potential. Self-governance in education by those participating in the learning process was the means to ensure that this potential would not be channeled into fulfilling the perceived needs of industry or the state. Education must be freed from the pressure to produce good citizens and workers in order to enable growing individuals to bring their own potential to expression. The task of schools must be to raise generations of children who can change society, drive its further evolution, not simply fit in and sustain it.

This was no utopian striving. The Waldorf School was not a training ground for a pre-conceived ideal society; the teachers were not considered to be initiates mandated by the spiritual world to raise a multitude of socially active adepts. What Steiner seems to have recognized was a shift in the relationship between the child and the societal forms within which he or she grows to maturity and then goes on to take responsibility.

The recognition of this shift is explicit in the first lecture Steiner gave to teachers. He begins by calling attention to the fact that each stage of human development has its own task. Education in the present epoch has a different task than it did in the preceding one. Most of what we know in education with its focus on logical reasoning, prescribed curricula and extrinsic forms of motivation and authority, however, is rooted in the past. What is the task for the present? What forms of education can plant and nourish the seeds of the future?

Anyone wishing to participate in shaping the governance structures of Waldorf schools must take these questions to heart.

Waldorf education is tasked with something new. It is not merely a variation on what we think education is and has been. Each Waldorf school represents the striving to free education from its servitude to the past and thus allow teachers to fully participate in the learning growing of today's children.

Whatever forms we adopt in our schools must reflect this striving. When Steiner obliged the teachers to develop governance and organizational forms that "would allow each teacher to become fully responsible"[3] it was with this end in mind. Each individual had to have the opportunity to become fully engaged, a participating co-creator of a new way of teaching. The school would have to be governed, organized, and administered in such ways that the teachers' insights into the learning and developmental needs of children could give it its direction. The biography of the school, the way it developed and changed would be based on this understanding.

Although the majority of our promotional literature celebrates the age and accomplishments of Waldorf education, there is something misleading in this. Waldorf education is young. Like all young endeavors, it is still in the process of finding its way. Its growing social acceptance and success in achieving mainstream educational goals has to some extent deadened awareness for its unique task. Although our society is obsessed with youthfulness, our view of education is disturbingly conservative. There is a widespread fear of change. This fear is also apparent in Waldorf education. The seemingly tried and true is more inviting than the new; accepted practice more appealing than innovation. In a school movement that was founded to re-chart education's course, this distaste for innovation is surprising. It seems that we are often more inclined to assimilate mainstream practices and objectives than to forge new paths out of our own understanding.

This hesitancy is also expressed in the choices we make concerning governance and organization and the forms we adopt to guide us in how we live and work together. If one examines these closely, one finds a multitude of practices that stifle change and a lack of dialogue that could help both teachers and parents better understand what they are experiencing with children. The two together prove fertile ground for a culture of distrust and isolation that once present in a school is very difficult to overcome.

Where distrust and isolation reign, self-governance is not possible. Self-governance is only possible in a culture of trust and collegiality, where there is a shared understanding of the task at hand. The shared understanding of the task is the starting-point for developing forms of self-governance. We develop such forms in order to enable ourselves to fulfill the task we have taken on. Today the challenge of institutional survival too often impinges on our ability to see the essentials of this task clearly. Steiner was fairly clear about it. In the first lecture he gave for the incoming faculty of the Stuttgart school he said in relation to the rhythms of breathing and sleeping: "All we can do is to use the time that human beings spend on the physical plane in such a way that they gradually become able to carry over into the spiritual world what they have experienced here; and that, in carrying it over, they can receive and bring back with them strength from the spiritual world which will help them to be true human beings in physical existence."[4] In 1923, during a conference for teachers at the Goetheanum in Dornach, he says it a bit differently: "Every education is self-education, and as teachers we can only provide the environment for children's self-education. We have to provide the most favorable conditions where, through our agency, children can educate themselves according to their own destinies."[5] The task we take on when we choose to become Waldorf teachers is to create learning environments in which children can practice the art of self-education, environments so richly contextualized that their experiences touch them and live on in them, imparting meaning to their learning. The challenge is to do this together, weaving through our shared work and striving for a contextual whole, where children encounter the presence of spiritually active individuals and the quality of community that is born of their intentional collaboration.

The forms we give ourselves can either help or hinder us in our striving to meet this challenge. The most productive will be those that scaffold us as we learn to better live with this task, that support us in becoming ever more able to practice an education of response and encounter that leads children from experience through imagination to understanding. The least productive will be those that subvert this striving to support other goals such as high enrollment, good test scores, or admission to elite colleges. Viable forms will support dialogue, streamline decision-making, and nurture initiative. They will support responsible participation and enable individuals to fully engage in their work. Their focus will be on sustainable institutional practices, pedagogical leadership through insight and initiative, and freely mandated accountability structures crafted to facilitate the smooth management of daily operations. Most important, all individuals working within the forms will know themselves and their work to be part of a greater whole, an educational adventure into the unknown, the constantly becoming.

2

A Creative Task

In the opening paragraphs of the *Foundations of Human Experience* (also translated as *Study of Man*), the introductory lectures given to the incoming teachers of the Stuttgart school, Rudolf Steiner speaks repeatedly of the nature of the task at hand. The term "task" is used fifteen times in the first three paragraphs. What is a task? It is something that needs to be done. We take on tasks, and although we may enjoy those that come our way, they are not recreational. They are done because they have to be done. "He was given the task of cleaning the old goat pen." "It was her task to shut the ducks in at night." Someone may be "taken to task" if they have not been doing the things they ought to have been doing. There are unpleasant tasks, necessary tasks, enjoyable tasks, obligatory tasks, tasks that we recognize and take on ourselves, tasks that others give us to do.

For Steiner the task of creating a new school based on the insights he had gained into human development through his anthroposophical research is a spiritual-moral task, one that places the teachers in a relationship of reciprocity with those spiritual beings most closely concerned with the child embarking on the journey through life. It is a task that entails continuing the work that these beings had begun before a child was born, and one that has to be done in such a way that the child's relation to the spiritual remains intact. It is an "important task," a "special task," one that should help in the further evolution of humanity. And it is a task that is specific to a given stage in humanity's development—the present stage.

A viable approach to developing and sustaining governance practices that help us achieve the qualities of learning and collaboration which Rudolf Steiner envisioned can only arise out of a deeply experienced sense of the task connected with this educational impulse.

One of the most striking examples of a learning encounter, which I believe illustrates this task, took place long before Rudolf Steiner and Emil Molt began planning the first Waldorf school.

The Example of Thomas Clarkson

During the second half of the 18th century, Britain began to awaken to the moral implications of the slave trade. One of the incidents that contributed to this awakening was the trial of the captain and officers of the *Zong*, a slave ship working between the West Indies and the west coast of Africa.[6] Although the trial received little attention at the time, it set the course for a series of events that would eventually lead to the abolition of slavery throughout the British empire.

The *Zong* had sailed from Africa to Jamaica with 440 slaves. Due to bad winds and long periods of calm the passage took more than twice as long as usual. The slaves, chained together in the hold, began to fall ill and die. The captain, Luke Collingwood, began to worry about his profit. Like other captains, he was paid a certain amount for each slave he delivered to the markets in Jamaica. For those who died on the voyage, he received no money. As the condition of the slaves grew increasingly dire, he came up with a plan to recap at least some money from the trip. Although the owners paid nothing for those slaves who had died along the way, the slaves were insured as cargo. If slaves died, due to "Perils [of the Sea] beyond the captain's control,"[7] they were covered by the insurance. He decided to jettison the sickest slaves, giving the reason that, due to length of the passage, the ship's water was running low. At first the crew was loathe to go along with Collingwood's decision, but under pressure from the captain they finally gave in. Over the course of the next days, a total of 133 slaves were cast into the ocean to drown. The last ten "sprang disdainfully from the grasp of their tyrants, defied their power, and, leaping into the sea, felt a momentary triumph in the embrace of death."[8]

The owners filed an insurance claim for the dead slaves, which the insurance company disputed. The case came to trial in 1783. Although the chief mate, moved by his conscience to right what he had come to think of as murder, testified that there was sufficient water on board at the time, the judge ruled in favor of the ship's owners. A further appeal did nothing to overturn the ruling. At no point did the court address the question of what in the eyes of some was an appalling case of mass murder.

Among those who were moved by the story of the *Zong's* slaves was a man named Dr. Peter Peckard, who was soon to become the vice-chancellor of Cambridge University. In 1785, he announced that the topic for the university's most prestigious Latin contest would be the question: *Anne liceat invitos in servitutem dare?* (Is it lawful to make slaves of others against their will?)

One of the young men who decided to participate in that year's contest was Thomas Clarkson. Clarkson had just finished training for the Anglican ministry and was waiting to take a position in a London church. He had two months to prepare and write his entry. "I had no motive but that which other young men in the University had on such occasions; namely the wish of ... obtaining literary honor."[9] But as he began to research the topic, he found himself confronted with a reality that moved him deeply. "In the daytime I was uneasy. In the night I had little rest. Sometimes I never closed my eye-lids for grief ... I always slept with a candle in the room, that I might rise out of bed and put down such thoughts as might occur to me in the night ... conceiving that no arguments of any moment should be lost in so great a cause."[10]

Clarkson won the first prize, read his essay for the academic elite of Britain and set out for London to begin his career as an Anglican clergyman. But as he rode towards the city, he found himself thinking neither of the prize nor of his future. What troubled him was the plight of the slaves. As he traveled along he went back over the interviews, the meetings and the arguments that he had developed in his paper. Finally, his feelings grew so intense that he sat down on the side of the road to think. "[...] I sat down disconsolate on the turf by the roadside and held my horse. Here a thought came into my mind, that if the contents of the Essay were true, it was time some person should see these calamities to their end."[11]

Clarkson went on to dedicate the rest of his life to the abolition of slavery, becoming the driving force in a movement that would write a new chapter in the growing awareness of the rights of the human individual, regardless of race. In an essay titled "Self-Reliance," Ralph Waldo Emerson wrote of him: "An institution is the lengthened shadow of one man ... the Reformation, of Luther; Quakerism, of Fox; Methodism, of Wesley; Abolition, of Clarkson. Scipio, Milton called 'the height of Rome'; and all history resolves itself very easily into the biography of a few stout and earnest persons."[12]

Thomas Clarkson's encounter with slavery epitomizes a certain quality of learning experience. In the process of gaining an understanding of the slave trade, the plight of the slaves and the inhumanity of the slavers, Clarkson met something that changed his life. He came to a quality of understanding so fraught with meaning that he was moved to act upon it. Slavery ceased to be something outside of him; he reached out, embraced it and allowed it to become part of himself. And as he pondered it, it came to life within him.

This is what Steiner hoped would take place in the Waldorf school: that children would encounter the lesson content in such a way that what they were meeting would come to life within them, that what they discovered through this would be able to grow and metamorphose as the children matured. Steiner developed an encounter-based approach to education — an approach that insured absolute freedom in the moment of learning. Content and process merge so that something new is made possible. Although all the children in a class are brought into a common encounter with any given phenomenon, what lives on in each child is unique.

This essential gesture of freedom rooted in the experience of meaning in the learning encounter was compromised from the beginning by the restrictions placed on the school in 1919 by the educational authorities. Over the course of the next years, Steiner would groan about the limitations, the schedule, the pressure to meet testing requirements. One wonders just what he would have done if they had not been there. Would he have chosen the school form that was prevalent in Germany in the early years of the twentieth century? Or would he have crafted a much more open, contextualized form, a form in which the quality of encounter was intensified? These are, in one way, moot questions as we have no indications as to what Steiner would have done. The schools that were inaugurated based on the work of the Stuttgart school during his life all took on the form that was allowed at the time. But we can ask whether we are still bound by the same restrictions. Is Waldorf education a historical model or a creative educational impulse, able to bring forth new forms to meet new needs?

How we answer this question impacts deeply the way we see our schools and the efforts we make to sustain and govern them. It affects the way we approach teacher-training, accreditation, learning goals, and so forth, not to mention the relationships between teachers, children, and parents. It colors the picture of human individuality that we present to the children growing up around us. Does the school resound with the creative striving to give a new educational impulse contextually appropriate form? Do children and parents experience the excitement of collegial initiative and exploration? Do they find a culture of earnest striving to better understand the developmental process and its signature in the individual child?

It seems evident that the core of any sustainable governance form in a Waldorf school must be the collaborative striving to better meet the needs of the children we encounter in the classrooms, in the workshops, in the gardens, at play. This is the core task of the school. Whatever arises out of this striving in the form of classroom practices, experiential approaches, subject content, and so forth, are but the outer expression of this inner activity.

Colleagues throughout the movement bear witness to the disappearance of this activity in many schools. Meetings are filled either with organizational or administrative details, or pass in a flurry of opinions concerning a child, a pedagogical issue, or even study material. Contributions from colleagues are either measured and weighed for their spiritual or political correctness, or disregarded as too emotionally charged; anthroposophical content tends to be so abstruse and abstract that people fall asleep. Differing opinions of what is truly Waldorf often clash, and different factions appear. The ability to come to inner as well as formal consensus dissipates. Inordinate amounts of time are then spent trying to come to acceptable compromises. As the meetings lose themselves in this maneuvering and negotiating, they are no longer able to give the school a sense of direction. Individual teachers find themselves forced into positions of authority; others feel that their ideas are not heard. Conflict arises, and then often simmers on due to unwillingness or inability to find ways to resolve it.

In the end, it is not only the individuals who suffer. What is lost is a sense of vitality throughout the whole school. Parents and students perceive it, Boards find themselves having to deal with issues that lie far beyond their purvey. Questions of accountability and decision-making, authority and policy begin to dominate the discussions. Paper trails become ever more important, attention is brought increasingly to focus on the outer aspects of institutional life. Volunteerism disappears, things are not done. People become afraid to step forward, to take a stand. Teachers withdraw into their classrooms, what was conceived as a collaborative, living whole becomes a collection of medieval kingdoms, in which "kings" and "queens" rule as they see fit. Policy and direction come from the strongest of these "monarchs" or groups of "monarchs." Teaching styles and focus differ from kingdom to kingdom; parents become more attached to "their" class teacher than they do to the school. Changes in curriculum tend to be *fait accompli*, with no lasting effect on the educational thrust of a school. Teachers start to battle one another for time and resources to teach their subjects the way they think they should be or the way some authority says they should be. What was conceived of as an integrated learning context deteriorates into various forms of fragmentation, where individual teachers have little or no living consciousness of what their colleagues are doing.

This is, of course, a far cry from what Steiner envisioned when he spoke of a teachers' republic.

The first step towards self-governance is the development of a culture of inquiry and interest concerning children's learning. Although it appears self-evident that the child's path of learning should stand at the center of our endeavors in Waldorf education, too often this is not reflected in practice. Behind every exploration of school development, every discussion of scheduling, every administrative policy, we should be able to feel the question: How does this impact children's learning? Does it help us create a more "Clarksonian" learning environment?

3

A Structure of Initiative

On the evening before the beginning of the first teachers' course in Stuttgart in 1919, Rudolf Steiner commented on the organizational structure that the school would need in order to succeed. These comments rightfully live on in the school movement today, often, however, giving rise to more questions than answers concerning the nature of governance and leadership within the dynamic learning organism of a Waldorf school. The picture becomes more complex and, for many people, confusing when, in addition to these rather cryptic remarks to the initial faculty members, we take into account Steiner's thoughts on social structures contained in his talks and writings on the threefold social order. It is here that he develops the ideas that underlie the vision of self-governance within institutions of the cultural sphere, an approach to organizational structure that has been practiced with varying degrees of success in Waldorf schools and other anthroposophical institutions throughout the world.

In a time of shifting paradigms, when traditional forms of leadership and social organization have proven themselves inadequate to the challenges at hand, self-governance appears as an ideal, something to be striven for. As with any ideal, it can only be realized through action. Self-governance becomes reality when a group of individuals practice it. This practice demands not only a certain level of maturity, self-discipline, and communication skills (both in speaking and in listening) from all involved; a clearly articulated shared vision of the challenge at hand is needed. The skills do not, however, come naturally. They must be learned. The way a school approaches the challenge of giving itself a structure will either support or place obstacles in the way of this learning process. In speaking to the first teachers, Steiner articulated the ideal. In his work on the threefold social order, we find an approach to understanding processes within a social organism that can guide us in developing ways of working together. Such an understanding enables us to bring the ideal into the realm of practice. Within a school, the unifying vision arises out of ongoing, shared work to better understand the nature of the growing child.

Remarks made on the evening of August 18, 1919, bear witness to how deeply Rudolf Steiner had taken Emil Molt's dream of a school to heart. This school would have to be "a true cultural deed" if it were to indeed lead to a renewal of contemporary spiritual life.[13] It was an opportunity to bring about reform, even a revolution, in education. How much lay on the shoulders of that first group of teachers! "The success of this cultural deed is in your hands....There is much resting on the success of this deed."[14]

The Waldorf school was born out of the chaos following WWI, and out of the collapse of the Threefold Movement. This grassroots movement, which led among other things to the first factory councils, in which workers participated in decision-making processes, had initially seen a good deal of support in southern Germany. Steiner made the rounds of the factories, speaking to large groups of workers and factory owners; he approached politicians; and he had volunteers handing out pamphlets on street corners. His book, *Towards Social Renewal,* published in 1919, went through four editions in the first year, selling some 30,000 copies in the first two months of publication.

The spring and summer of 1919 brought weeks of intense work. Both in Switzerland and in southern Germany, Steiner plunged into the social turmoil that followed the collapse of the German war effort, offering an independent voice between the great ideological powers of capitalism and communism. His public statements began with the fall of the imperial German government in November 1918, when he started to speak openly about the war and the machinations of power that had brought it about. His lectures of this time resonated with what some listeners would call a "Wachruf," a wake-up call. The old order had collapsed (in the first weeks of November 1918, four kings, nine Grand Dukes, and twelve princes abdicated, giving up not only the right to rule, but most of their properties). Workers Councils were being formed throughout Germany, and the established political parties were fighting to gain power. Leftist elements in the Workers' Movement had tried to take control of the government by force in Berlin; there was street fighting in many of the major German cities.

It was into this maelstrom that Steiner entered when he returned to Germany from Switzerland in the spring of 1919. At the urging of Emil Molt, Hans Kuehn, Roman Boos, and others, Steiner had agreed to spearhead a grassroots campaign to realize the threefold ideas in the formation of the new German government. To this end he had written "A Call to Action," which was signed by many people of all stations in life, and the above-mentioned book *Towards Social Renewal.* The "Call to Action" had been in circulation for a number of weeks, and Molt, Kuehn, and the Threefold Committee members had been active in the Stuttgart area. With Steiner's arrival, and the arrival of young enthusiastic anthroposophists from throughout Europe, the Threefold Movement picked up steam and seemed for a time to be able to create a space within which all the various factions could meet and move ahead. Steiner felt most supported by the factory workers, who seemed to be willing to act first and work out the details as they went along.

This is a theme that surfaces repeatedly in Steiner's talks on social issues. The threefold approach is not an abstract system with answers for all the details of social life. It is a way of understanding how the different parts of a social organism function and what allows them to function in a productively collaborative manner. Steiner saw the Threefold Movement as a spontaneous, self-organizing movement. Once the general direction was clear, further ideas would arise out of the work.

The movement, however, was short-lived. By June, Steiner had begun to see the writing on the wall. He didn't give up, however, but continued to work closely with the workers and the factory councils. Resistance grew. The socialist parties had begun to fear the erosion of their influence over the workers and had intensified their propaganda. The lack of political abilities among the volunteers left the full weight of the work on Steiner's own shoulders. But what was most difficult was the realization that most of his listeners were not able to really understand the import of the relationships described in the ideas of the threefold social order. "In the proletariat the destructive superstition has taken root that all rights and all cultural life of natural necessity arise out of economic forms. Large circles of non-proletarians have also fallen prey to this way of thinking. What has developed over the last few centuries as a historical phenomenon: the dependence of the legal sphere and the cultural sphere on the economic sphere is seen as a natural necessity. No one sees the truth: this dependence has driven humankind into a catastrophe; many people believe that all we need is a different economic form, one which will give birth to new legal and cultural forms."[15] This way of thinking combined with a deep sense of obedience to those in positions of authority made it impossible to bring to life the kinds of initiatives that could have led to the realization of a network of autonomous, self-administering councils in the three fields of social life: the legal sphere, the economic sphere, and the cultural sphere. And although the work towards a threefold social order continued both in Germany and Switzerland, in August Rudolf Steiner turned his attention to other tasks, the primary one being the preparations for the opening of the first Waldorf school.

Both historically and spiritually, it is impossible to imagine the Waldorf School without the threefold social impulse. In fact, Waldorf education is the only part of Threefold Movement of 1918/1919 to survive.

A number of people related that they had never seen Rudolf Steiner as fresh and full of vitality as at the beginning of the fourteen-day course for the teachers of the Waldorf School and again at the ceremonial opening of the school some three weeks later.[16] The opening of the school marked the beginning of a new chapter in the development of the anthroposophical work. In the hectic spring and summer of 1919, Steiner had worked tirelessly to awaken people to the possibility of social renewal through concrete action. Now he was immersed in the realization of such an initiative. His commitment to the work of Waldorf education remained strong throughout the last years of his life, a commitment that epitomizes his approach to social change: it is to be achieved through individual action, individual initiative born of practical idealism.

This is what rings through his words to the teachers as they gathered to prepare for the short intense training that preceded the opening of the school. No abstract system of schooling could bring about a paradigmatic shift in education; it would take a new, evolving understanding of the nature of the incarnating child and a strong sense of individual commitment to bring this understanding into practice in the daily meeting between teacher and child. Each teacher would have to put everything in the pot, success would rest on his or her ability to realize the ideal, not to fulfill a predetermined educational program but to bring his or her spiritual capacities to bear fully on the task ahead. Children cannot grow to freedom, creativity and responsibility unless they are surrounded by adults who practice these capacities.

Keeping this in mind, what Steiner said about the organization of the new school becomes clearer. The challenge of practical idealism, action born of ethical individualism, lies in the dynamic nature of the realization of an ideal. Ideals are born of the spirit and light up within human consciousness as a possibility. Much work lies between the recognition of this possibility and its coming into being in the world. The organizational structure of the school would have to be one that placed no unnecessary obstacles in the path of this realization; it would have to be one that would help the individuals involved become increasingly capable of both realizing their own ideals and supporting others in the realization of their ideals. It would have to be a social structure that nurtured initiative and nourished enthusiasm for the task at hand.

"Thus we will give the school an administrative, not a governmental organizational structure, and manage it in a republican manner. In a true teachers' republic we won't be able to simply lean back on the directives that come from above, but we will have to bring to bear what gives each of us the possibility to take full responsibility for what we have to do. Each must be fully responsible."[17]

This short sketch of what is both a governance model (teacher's republic) and an organizational structure (administrative, not governmental) is as inextricably tied to the birth and development of Waldorf education as are the fourteen lectures that followed. Like them it also contains riddles that can only be solved in practice.

4

The Early Years

The Waldorf School was the first cultural initiative to grow out of the anthroposophical movement. Although it was explicitly not an anthroposophical school, it was just as explicitly created with the intent of letting the quality of insight that can flow out of anthroposophical practice bear fruit in the society at large. From the very beginning, the Waldorf School was an emerging reality, an endeavor that took on form as it grew, a learning organism that let itself be guided by experience.

Waldorf education evolved in the dialogue between teachers, students and, until he died in 1925, Rudolf Steiner. It was only when he was confined to his bed and unable to return to work with the teachers that Steiner placed the future of the school in the hands of the faculty. One of his last communications with the school begins: "Not to be with you all means great deprivation to me. And so I must hand over to your care the important decisions, which I have naturally shared with you since the opening of the school. It is a time when destiny tests us. I am with you in thought."[18] He follows this with a verse, which is as relevant to our work as it was to that of the first teachers:

May active power of thought unite us,
Since parted in space we needs must be.
May what has been achieved so far,
Strongly work among the teachers of this school.
May it live within their counseling,
Since the counselor, who would so gladly come,
Has wings no longer free to fly.

The Waldorf School specifically and Waldorf education in general did not come into existence fully formed. It grew out of the striving to give a new understanding of human development practical manifestation. It was a shared striving; the forms that arose came about through the practical, day-to-day work of teaching and observing the learning child. The driving force in this development was the dialogue between those who were working together to bring it about.[19] Steiner accompanied the process with interest, engagement, personal intention and concern. For him the Waldorf school was always "a child in need of special care."

Placing the responsibility for the important decisions in the life of the school in the hands of the teachers was not something Steiner seems to have done lightly. The letter quoted above was written just over two weeks before his death. His concern was not unfounded. Over the years he had experienced time and again the challenges and impasses that arose as the faculty struggled to work together to bring this school into existence. And he was often quite open with his rebukes. Sometimes these were directed at the faculty as a whole as in the teachers' meeting on October 15, 1922: "If we only had a guarantee that you people will realize once more that you have to follow the Waldorf school principles. If only we had a guarantee of that! But I see no sign of it…. I miss the fire which ought to be in it. There is no fire but apathy. There is a certain laziness there. Our original intentions hardly come to expression at all.… I always take for granted that the college consists of people who have ability.… But people are asleep and function as though their eyes and ears were shut. I am not reproaching a single teacher, but routine methods are gaining ground."[20] At other times he spoke to individuals. But whether to individuals or to the group, his words are direct, free of rancor, and leave no question as to their meaning. Most important, they are spoken with the school in mind, the shared ideal, the shared endeavor. His reproaches have nothing to do with personal antipathy; his praise is equally free of personal sympathy. What binds him to the individuals gathered as teachers in the Waldorf School is not a sense of like or dislike. The college is not a community of friends. It is a collaborative effort to bring to fruition a radical departure from conventional schooling. When the shared consciousness of this striving weakens, when "routine methods" creep in, it is not the personal harmony among the teachers that is at stake, it is the spiritual reality of Waldorf education.

Many schools today would like to have someone like Steiner to give them guidance. It is not only hard to keep this educational ideal alive within oneself in the tides of daily life; it is even harder to keep it alive in working together as colleagues. Who of us has achieved such a mastery of our work that gives us the right to pass judgments on the work of others? Perhaps one of the greatest strengths of collaborative governance is the sense of humility it instills in one. Yet no school can exist and flourish without guidance, without clarity among the colleagues of its principles and the ability to speak of the times when we fall short of our ideals. The fear of disharmony is not the same as professional humility. Spades must be called spades. Straight speaking, directness, and a practiced lack of ambiguity are essential if a group of adults are to share responsibility for something that is constantly in a process of being re-created.

Rudolf Steiner visited the Waldorf School as often as he could from 1919 until 1923. When he was there, he visited classrooms and spoke with the students; consulted with individual teachers; met with the faculty; and gave lectures for the teachers, the parents, and the public. The transcripts of the teachers' meetings offer insight into the internal dynamics of these first years of Waldorf education. It was not easy going. The faculty struggled not only with the pedagogical aspects of their work, but also with the challenges of collaboration and self-governance. Rudolf Steiner was present at seventy teachers' meetings; the work of the teachers and questions of governance and administration were spoken of explicitly in twenty-one of them.

Surprisingly, the idea of a weekly faculty meeting does not seem to have come from Steiner. On September 25, 1919, shortly after the school first opened, during a meeting that dealt with everything from student supplies to religious lessons, in the middle of a discussion of Roman history, a teacher said: "We want to have a meeting every week to discuss pedagogical questions, so we can all benefit from one another's experiences." Steiner replied: "That can certainly happen, and it is something that would be welcomed. It would have to be kept very republican." The rest of the first year passed with little mention of the working of the faculty. On June 9, Steiner suggested that the teachers keep a common "Golden Book" of observations and interesting occurrences and on June 14, he remarked: "Another thing that would be extremely good to do, if it can be managed, would be to discuss individual children as such, either in groups or separately, and make them the concern of the whole college. This strikes me as very desirable. But you have to give it your interest."

Towards the end of the school year, on July 30, 1920, a longer discussion ensued concerning college membership. This discussion is significant. It was triggered by questions concerning a practical arts teacher who had been hired from the ranks of workers at the Waldorf-Astoria factory to take on certain classes. He was admitted to the faculty meetings before it became clear whether he was capable of becoming a "Waldorf" teacher. At this juncture it had become clear that this did not seem to be the case and he would have to be asked to leave. (He was asked to leave that day. The discussion concerning this step is very instructive. It is never easy to let someone go.) Steiner remarked: "It cannot be taken for granted that all the specialist teachers should be on the college. There ought to be a core faculty consisting of class teachers and older specialist teachers, and also a larger, or expanded faculty." This is the first time that such a differentiation is mentioned. Steiner uses here the term *engeres Kollegium* (core faculty), as opposed to an *erweitertes Kollegium* (full faculty).

He goes on to say: "Only the principal teachers belong on the core faculty, and those among them who are actually teaching, not those on leaves of absence. Basically, those on the core faculty should be those who have been at the school from the beginning and, among the teachers who came later, those whom we would have wished to have had at last year's course. Whoever joins us as a genuine teacher has always been considered. To be on the core faculty they must in the first place be actually teaching, and secondly they must be real teachers." In reply to a remark from Mrs. Molt that she certainly didn't fulfill those conditions, Steiner said that there are exceptions: herself, Marie Steiner, Emil Molt. If things are spoken about they become clear. Baravalle had only been there briefly, but also belonged in the core faculty meeting.

Who belongs in the core faculty? Steiner is very clear, one could say emphatic: real teachers who are actually teaching. But then there are exceptions—the Molts, Marie Steiner, Steiner himself. The core faculty should be made up of the teachers who have been at the school from the beginning, but can also include new teachers who "we would have liked to have at last year's course."

What seems apparent is that Steiner acted in a completely situational manner, making decisions based on the reality of the situation and the people involved. The working principle behind the work of the core faculty: the development of the school in a manner that reflects the spiritual understanding of child development and learning. This necessitates that the strongest voices in the school be those who are, in fact, teaching and through teaching, learning. This working principle is, however, not a Mosaic reality. It is not legalistic. It is the working reality of the core faculty, not the procedural regulation of an institution. Yes, those on the core faculty should be teachers, but there are exceptions, individuals who are so deeply connected to the existence of the school and the educational impulse that they too should be able to participate. Who are these people? They will be different from school to school. Can they be parents? There does not seem to be any reason why this should not be a possibility.

Steiner's antipathy towards any tendency to codify living relationships becomes even more apparent in the meetings held at the beginning of the second school year, 1920/21. The financial situation of the school had become somewhat precarious in the second half of the first year, although the number of children continued to climb. This led to tension between the school and the Board of the Waldorf-Astoria factory of which Emil Molt was the director. The tension came to a head at the beginning of the new school year. The teachers drew up a statute re-defining the school's relationship to the cigarette factory. In this document Steiner was named as the "School Director." It was also stated that the teachers would no longer be engaged by the factory. Emil Molt spoke at length about the situation in the factory, his own situation regarding both the factory and the core faculty, and about the statute. Steiner pointed out that there was no question of his taking on the position of director and that there appeared to be underlying issues at hand that were not being addressed. The teachers had always been vetted and chosen by the core faculty, considerations from the side of the Waldorf-Astoria were heard also, but the considerations of the core faculty took precedence. One of the teachers said: "I made the statute to bring form into our working together. It is important that the college be independent in spiritual matters, like a corporation of spiritual workers, and the appointing and dismissing of teachers belongs to this. What concerned me was the finding of the right form to express Dr. Steiner's position vis-a-vis the college." To which Steiner responded: "I find it hard to come to terms with a statute because statutes mean nothing to me. We can only take each day as it comes. Statutes are necessary when the outside world is concerned, so that it looks like something. That is why I always find it so hard to come to terms with a statute because they mean so little to me. I don't think a statute can make any appreciable difference to anything…"

The next day Rudolf Steiner spoke to the teachers about how he viewed the inner aspects of his relationship to them and their work. He began by stating the connection between this work and the anthroposophical movement: "Where things connected with our spiritual movement are concerned — and the management of the Waldorf School, insofar as it is a spiritual matter and in-sofar as it is a pedagogical and didactic matter belonging to the teachers' conference, is connected with our anthroposophical movement—where matters of this kind are concerned I feel towards you as an esotericist, and shall never be able to feel otherwise." The way in which an esotericist shares insights with others is not based on authority as we generally understand it. It is based on "a kind of acknowledgement that a source exists from which these things can be drawn." "[…] the person who speaks of these things does not speak in such a way that what is said shall be accepted on authority in the ordinary sense." If this were the case, what is passed on would not be able to have the appropriate effect on those who hear it. The relationship between the spiritual teacher and those who choose to listen to what is given must be different. "There must be the kind of relationship in which everything that is said is received by the hearers of their own free will; nothing may be permitted to depend on the will of the speaker, but everything must depend simply and solely on the will of the listeners."

Rudolf Steiner's understanding of his role in the school gives us some insight into how he envisioned leadership and authority arising in this new stage of human evolution. If he was to have any authority in the school, it could only come from the recognition that what he brought was of some value to the teachers working with him. His authority could not be institutionalized based on a statute or position. It could only arise out of the will of the teachers to follow his guidance. In no way could he impinge on their freedom. "If we work as teachers should, then the very thing that will bring progress into the world out of the realms of the spirit must on no account be received by way of any soul-compelling authority. Ideally everything must be received on the strength of goodwill and the listener's insight and feeling that the person who is speaking has something to say…. The whole relationship must be based on speaking without asserting authority and listening born of free will."

He was emphatic that the only healthy, and healing, form of collaborative relationship would be one that developed based on such an understanding. Leaders receive authority through the spiritual acknowledgement of those who choose to work with them. This shift in the definition of authority is fundamental for an understanding of the nature of governance in the Waldorf School then, and in the schools today. The respect for individual freedom that lies at its core should not, however, be equated with personal license, the notion that everyone is free to do what he or she wants. No social or cultural endeavor can succeed without leadership; the choice to follow must, however, be born of freedom.

Differentiating between core faculty and full faculty consultations was voiced briefly in the faculty meeting on November 15, 1920, when Rudolf Steiner asked the gathered members of the core faculty if there was anything they had to discuss before the rest of the teachers joined them. Then, on March 23, 1921, in light of a discussion concerning the formation of an extra student eurythmy group, he pointed out that such things which had an impact on the principles of the school should be discussed in the faculty meetings, not simply decided and implemented outside of them.

The third school year began in June 1921, with only a one-week break following the end of the previous year. The school now had 540 students in 15 classes. The faculty had grown to 30. Throughout the course of the next year, Rudolf Steiner made a number of remarks expressing his disappointment in how things were developing. "There is not sufficient liveliness in the instruction. In most classes, you seem to be having difficulty working with the children…. When we do not teach efficiently, we burden the students. We should avoid wasting time for that reason. We should not do everything as though we had an endless amount of time…. The individual teachers need to communicate with one another. The fact that there is no communication can at best be a question of lack of time, but, in principle, you always need to discuss things with one another." Many of these comments are concerned with questions of collaboration and colleagueship. Steiner sensed that the connections between teachers and between the teachers and the students were being strained, that the lessons were losing their liveliness.

Three aspects of collegial work were highlighted during the year. The first concerned Baravalle's doctoral dissertation on teaching mathematics and physics, which had been published that summer. Rudolf Steiner mentioned it in a number of different contexts. The one that interests us in this exploration was voiced during the conference on September 11, 1921. Steiner emphasized the importance of studying the work of one's colleagues. "I would like to mention that there is an esoteric significance in enlivening instruction when a lively interest exists for the work done by members of the faculty…. The entire faculty is enlivened when you take an interest in some original work by a colleague…. The fact is that the spiritual forces within the faculty carry the faculty through a communal inner experience." Three things come to expression here. The first concerns the individual. Baravalle's dissertation was a work of originality, the expression of his inner, spiritual activity. It was worth reading, but, more important, the interest of his colleagues for this work would enliven their work. This is the second aspect that Rudolf Steiner calls to the faculty's attention. The third concerns the nature of the teaching community and what can carry it. It is "the spiritual forces within the faculty" that, when shared, can give them the kind of inner experience of community that will enable them to meet their work in a lively, creative manner. It is not enough to have originality in individual members of the faculty. If it is not shared, this spiritual activity cannot bear fruit, cannot build and sustain community. Individual spiritual activity, when taken up with interest by colleagues contributes to the weaving of a community of spirit—the strongest of all forms of community.

The issue of community building arose again in a long discussion during the teachers' meeting on November 16. The teachers expressed the desire to have a form of Sunday service for the faculty. Steiner's initial response was quite positive: "Of course, something beautiful could come from that. I could easily imagine a unified striving coming from it." Then he raised the question of who would hold such a service. Coming to a decision about this would only be possible if they had "a deeply unified will." Although the teachers do not seem to have given much importance to the question of who would hold the service, Steiner obviously did. One of the teachers suggested that it be done by one of the three colleagues responsible for holding the children's service. Steiner replied: "Only if it were perfectly clear that that is acceptable. A service is either simply a question of form, in which case you could do it together, or it is a ritual act, and you have to look more seriously at it. In that case, you can have no secret enemies."

At this point the discussion shifts. After listening to another teacher speak about the service, Steiner admits to being lost, unable to understand anything anymore. Unfortunately, we do not have any record of what the teacher said. Working back from Steiner's recorded words, we can safely assume that he raised the question of a sacrament as opposed to an esoteric ritual. Here I will only call attention to one aspect of what follows. Steiner does not seem to have had reservations about considering such a ritual for the faculty. He does, however, point out that a group can carry an esoteric form only if it is united. Something that requires "such careful creation might be too difficult to create out of the

faculty and too difficult to care for within the faculty as a whole."
What would happen in the future? "Let us assume that you are
all in agreement. Then, we could only accept new colleagues into
the faculty who also agree. It is only possible to esoterically unite
people who choose to be united in a specific esoteric form." If
there were faculty members who preferred to celebrate in a non-
esoteric manner another form would have to be created for them.
This would exist "in contrast to the esoteric."

The whole question of esoteric studies and rituals was a sore
point for Steiner. Although he had tried to place esoteric schooling on a new footing, reckoning with discreteness born of individual freedom and insight rather than with the traditional code
of silence inherent in ancient esoteric communities, he had finally suspended all ritual esoteric work because of what he perceived
was a lack of earnestness and understanding. The two things he
found most devastating were the forming of cliques and the public distortion of details not meant for public consumption. No
form of esoteric act, whether it be the recitation of mediations or
the creation of symbolic rituals, can serve to unite those who do
not choose from the depths of their souls to be united.

Collegial working was spoken of explicitly once more that
year, on January 14, 1922. In the middle of a discussion concerning specific children and how best to carry them, Steiner said:
"Work together willingly! Understand your colleagues in the
faculty! Things are getting better. You need to be interested in
speaking about pedagogical questions. We should need no major
preparations for discussing pedagogy. Outline it, like going for a
walk, then follow that with a fruitful discussion."

The fourth school year was the most difficult. In the introduction to the first complete publication of the teachers' meetings in 1975, Erich Gabert wrote: "Right at the beginning of the
year, before classes began, for the first time dark clouds appeared

on the horizon. The storm broke and continued until February 1923. Rudolf Steiner's words were sharp, scolding. But then, to counter the dark mood that had arisen among the teachers, he gave seven special presentations, each of which threw light on a specific aspect of education. At times they took up an entire faculty meeting. With enormous effort, he managed to lift up what was in danger of foundering."

Much of Steiner's concern had to do with what he described as the breakdown of relationships between the teachers and the students. This was especially apparent in the upper grades. A number of students had to be expelled from the then eleventh grade. The mood among the teachers was also strained. Cliques formed, and it became increasingly difficult for the teachers to come to consensus. Questions of trust arose between the faculty and the individual who was carrying most of the school's administrative functions. Finally, a request was made to restructure the school's administrative work. This led to the establishment of a committee taxed with the responsibility for specific areas of the school's management.

The transcripts do not shed much light on the specific events leading up to the re-structuring. Steiner seems to have been aware of the perceived problem and to have already given it some thought. The discussions that accompanied the creation of what might be termed a mandated executive management team shed light on a number of questions: the manner in which Steiner approached collaborative decision-making, the seemingly archetypal challenge of sustaining unity among faculty members, and the use of democratic forms in the decision-making process. They also show how important it was for Steiner that things be thought through to their logical conclusions. He had no patience for the tendency to politely skirt around unspoken conflicts. If it was alive in the hearts and souls of the teachers, it had to be placed openly on the table. "In the realm of anthroposophy, honesty, not intransigence, should rule. That is what I am asking you to do, at least here at the seat of the Waldorf School, to begin for once to seriously stand upright, so that we do not fall into an atmosphere where we shut our eyes to the disharmony, but, instead, honestly say what we have to say."

We can also learn from the process by which the committee was formed. At Steiner's suggestion, the faculty named a committee to think through the situation and make a proposal to the faculty. This proposal was discussed, and then voted on. Steiner allowed no substantive changes to be made to the proposal brought by the committee. In a first step, the faculty identified and mandated colleagues who they trusted were able to give the question due consideration. The proposition brought back to the group was not allowed to be tinkered with before it was brought to a vote; in fact, the attempt by two teachers to amend the proposal was met with strong disapprobation. In the discussion, Steiner tried again and again to have those who had brought the counterproposal voice their reasons for doing so. When they were unable or unwilling to do so, and then withdrew the amendment, he appears not to have been able to fathom what they were thinking. Either one takes what one proposes seriously and is willing to voice the reasons for it or one remains silent. Compromise or retreat in this situation is counter-productive. The only thing that is important is that the truth comes to light.

How timely these words seem now, some ninety years later!

Another aspect that is important to note is the use of a small mandate group to support the cultivation of unity among a large faculty. We are often tempted to approach this problem from the other side. If dissent and distrust are growing in a faculty, many colleagues feel it is important to have everyone involved in everything. There is clearly a social riddle here that is worth pondering.

5

Governance in a Learning Community

Governance is an elusive term. In general usage, it usually indicates a relationship of authority between those who govern and those who are governed. The Oxford Dictionary definition of the word refers the reader to the verb govern which has as its first definition: "To rule with authority, esp. that of a sovereign; to direct and control the affairs of (a people, etc.) whether despotically or constitutionally; to regulate the affairs of (a body of men)." The verb, which is derived from the Greek *kubernan* meaning "to steer" made its way into the English language by way of Latin and Old French in the middle of the thirteenth century. The Greeks had already emancipated the word from its original concrete "to steer a ship," and begun to use it in a more abstract sense meaning "to guide." In its travels across Europe it lost its philosophical nuances and by the time it reached England it had acquired the meanings of "to control" or "to rule."

This is not what we are striving for. A Waldorf school cannot look to the past for guidance in understanding the nature of its governance. It must look to the future. And in doing so, recognize the qualities and functions that will allow us to practice the capacities that are needed to create and sustain a more human future. Governance structures worthy of the ideal that lies at the core of the Waldorf educational impulse have one thing in common: They are there to support the striving individual. They are, in the best sense of the word, learning structures, as opposed to control structures.[21]

The development of such structures—structures that support us in becoming better able to meet the needs of the children entrusted to us—requires a complete re-thinking of our notion of governance, including the vocabulary we use to describe it. Control, power, and accountability (at least as it is usually used today) have no place in a discussion of governance forms in a Waldorf school. These terms reflect an understanding of governance that was made manifest in what Steiner termed a governmental approach, an approach he refused to practice either in the first Waldorf school or in his other social endeavors.

What are the words that allow us to capture the essence of an approach to governance that is worthy of what we are striving for in education? Such an approach must be participatory, allowing individuals throughout the school community to engage themselves in the life and well-being of the school in a manner that allows them to grow as individuals. It must be an approach that encourages initiative and fosters dialogue. And it must be dynamic in the sense that it must be able to change and grow as the school does and as the abilities of the individuals involved in the school change.

The prevalence of fear in many discussions concerning school governance today is striking. It exists not only between the various "stakeholder" groups, but also within these groups. Teachers may express fear concerning the impact parents or a Board could have on the future development of a school, but when one participates in their meetings with one another it often is apparent that this fear is something systemic. One can experience it among parents, who worry that the cultural choices other parents make will have an adverse affect on their children; between parents and children; in conversations between teachers and parents, who worry that either one might find fault with the other; and even between teachers and children.

The degree to which fear has become an intrinsic aspect of most, if not all, social interaction today, is something that deserves not to be overlooked. What are we afraid of? One another? Ourselves? Whatever the answer, one thing is certain: Fear is not a viable basis for productive governance. Collaboration within a structure that was designed to protect special interests or control outcomes is not possible.

The approach we are looking for must be rooted in a deep sense of trust, not a shapeless, inconsequential abstract principle that is bandied about as a slogan, but a deep, creative, engaged commitment: to the spiritual that strives to bring itself to expression in the other; to the spiritual that brings forth the world that sustains us and gives us the gift of ourselves; to the spiritual that comes to me as challenge from the circumstances of life, enabling me to become more upright, more focused, more human. It must be based on the practiced interest in the other, rather than on the desire to protect one's own self-interest.

Conversations with teachers and parents in Waldorf schools point to a sense of personal inadequacy as the greatest source of fear. Teachers often feel inadequate to live up to what seems to be expected of them; few parents have a deep sense of certainty in relation to the challenges of parenting. Both parents and teachers voice feeling judged by the other. To some extent, this is due to a lack of clarity about what a Waldorf school is and the kind of learning environment it is trying to create. Marketing Waldorf schools as academically rigorous, college preparatory schools has affected what parents expect from a Waldorf school.

Teachers often find themselves bringing the same approaches into the classroom they had once hoped to overcome by committing themselves to Waldorf education.

Clarity about school identity, learning goals and curriculum is an essential factor in overcoming the fear that has become so prevalent in our schools. Forms of open dialogue between parents and teachers are equally needed. Only when we address the underlying causes of the fear and the distrust it breeds will we be able to overcome the prevailing tendency in governance to fall back on structures that aim to secure control. The governance structures that seem most worthy of our striving are such that would encourage the qualities of interaction that enable individuals to support one another in becoming more capable of living up to the tasks posed by education today—both as teachers and as parents.

Why is such a re-thinking of the goals of governance in a Waldorf school helpful? It gives us a road map to both assess the current structures and to envision new ones. It gives us a way to focus the discussion. If we are clear about what our governance structures should make possible, it is easier to find the forms we need. A conscious approach to school governance is only possible if there is clarity about what we are striving to achieve by developing forms of self-governance that can meet the varied needs and demands of a school community.

When Rudolf Steiner worked with the teachers of the first Waldorf school to find and develop forms and structures that would serve that school as it grew, he did so with a clear end in mind. He wanted forms that were livable, workable; forms that could be affirmed and upheld by the teachers who were committed to bringing this new form of education into the world. They weren't based on an abstract model or system, nor were they derived from distant principles. They were hands-on structures, developed out of the expressed needs of the situation. They were necessary structures.

Most of all, they were not seen as static structures. Schools change and grow. The structures must do so also. Governance is a living conceptual reality, not an abstract system. This is often difficult to realize in practice. We have a tendency to want to create structures that can live on into the future, memorializing and ritualizing a certain understanding of how things should be. Governance documents often reflect this striving, setting out in great detail not only the various bodies and committees and how they should function, but also the philosophical intent behind them. In the attempt to get everything right, and insure that no part can be instrumentalized, the documents become needlessly cumbersome, and through their exaggerated attention to the microscopic details become an obstacle to the life they profess to enable. A butterfly is only a being of light as long as it is free to live in the movement of the light-filled air. When captured and pinned in a box, it may remain a thing of beauty, but it loses the very qualities that made it so enchanting.

This is true of everything alive. And nothing is more alive than the intentional striving of individuals to create a social context in which the needs of another can be met creatively. The crafting of governance structures that enable them to live up to this striving must reflect the living character of their intent.

It is probably time to re-conceive the idea of governance. Although we have not yet reached the goal of individual development that would allow us to practice an anarchic approach based purely on ethical individualism, we cannot allow ourselves to be forced back into forms of institutional dependency that arise out of control and command structures. Governance structures always support certain kinds of social interaction, while hindering others. In addressing the question of governance in the context of the educational environment we hope to cultivate, it makes sense to become aware of which kinds of social interaction we wish to foster.

In developing the ideas expressed both here and in my work with schools in various parts of the world, I have worked from certain assumptions in this regard. I have assumed that the social environment should be one of intentional, explorative dialogue rather than one of dogmatism; that it should challenge each individual to be more interested in the process of becoming than in having become something; that it requires teachers and parents to understand their tasks and responsibilities and to wish to live up to the expectations inherent in them; that it is imbued by a shared, basic commitment to Steiner's work and the interest to better understand it. I have also assumed that the only social environment suitable for a school is one that can be called a learning environment, a social context that supports and encourages the practice of individual learning. And, as was mentioned above, I have assumed that the only viable form of social interaction as we head into the future is one that consciously embraces what I would like to call engaged trust and intentional tolerance.

Perhaps the best-known practitioner of these last two qualities was the Indian activist and statesman Mohandas Gandhi. Born in 1869 to a family of some consequence in one of the small, feudal states of western India, Gandhi grew to become the symbol of non-violent resistance to oppression for people throughout the world. Perhaps most importantly, he extended "the principle of non-violence from the individual to the social and the political plane,"[22] and in doing so laid the foundations of a social culture based on trust rather than on fear.

In fact, he viewed fear as the greatest impediment along the path to the recognition of individual truth and justice.

No government should enact laws aimed at instilling fear in its citizens. No citizen should silence his or her conscience out of fear of retaliation.

In the last lecture Rudolf Steiner gave for the teachers of the first Waldorf School, he points to Gandhi as a model for the kind of social engagement the school needed to succeed:

Teachers ought to be conscious, especially nowadays, of their great social task; they should, in fact, meditate on this task. The teacher, above all others, should be deeply permeated with awareness of the great needs of modern civilization. I will give you an example of what is needed in order to adopt the right attitude in our civilization today.

You have all heard of Mahatma Gandhi who, since the war, or really since 1914, has set in motion a movement to liberate India from English rule. Gandhi's activities began in South Africa with the aim of helping the Indians who were living there under appalling conditions, and for whose emancipation he did a great deal before 1914. Then he returned to India and sparked a movement for liberation there. I shall speak today only of what took place when the final verdict was passed on Mahatma Gandhi, and omit the court proceedings leading up to it. I would like to speak only of the last act in the drama, as it were, that took place between him and his judge. Gandhi had been accused of stirring up the Indian people against British rule in order to make India independent. Being a lawyer, he conducted his own defense and had not the slightest doubt that he would be condemned. In his speech—I cannot quote the actual words—he spoke more or less to the following effect, "My Lords, I beg of you to condemn me in accordance with the full strength of the law. I am perfectly aware that in the eyes of British law in India my crime is the gravest one imaginable.

I do not plead any mitigating circumstances; I beg of you to condemn me with the full strength of the law. I affirm, moreover, that my condemnation is required not only in obedience to the principles of outer justice but to the principles of expediency of the British government. For if I were to be acquitted I should feel it incumbent upon me to continue to propagate the movement, and millions of Indians would join it. My acquittal would lead to results that I regard as my duty." The contents of this speech are very characteristic of what lives and weaves in our time. Gandhi says he must of necessity be condemned, and declares it his duty to continue the activity for which he is to be condemned. The judge replied, "Mahatma Gandhi, you have rendered my task of sentencing you immeasurably easier, because you have made it clear that I must of necessity condemn you. It is obvious that you have transgressed against British law, but you and all those present will realize how hard it will be for me to sentence you. It is clear that a large portion of the Indian people looks upon you as a saint, as one who has taken up his task in obedience to the highest duties devolving upon humanity. The judgment I shall pass on you will be looked upon by the majority of the Indian people as the condemnation of a human being who has devoted himself to the highest service of humanity. Clearly, however, British law must in all severity be put into effect against you. You would regard it as your duty, if you were acquitted, to continue tomorrow what you were doing yesterday. We on our side have to regard it as our most solemn duty to make that impossible. I condemn you in the full consciousness that my sentence will in turn be condemned by millions. I condemn you while admiring your actions, but condemn you I must." Gandhi's sentence was six years at hard labor. You could hardly find a more striking example of what is characteristic of our times."[23]

In thinking about the development of spiritually, that means practically, sustainable governance forms, it makes sense to take a closer look at Gandhi's work.

—

The Example of Gandhi

Mohandas Gandhi is one of those individuals to whom many people today like to profess closeness without, however, being inclined to risk the comfort of their middle class lives to walk in his footsteps. We have a similar relationship to figures like Rosa Parks, Martin Luther King, or Thomas Clarkson. Gandhi's beginnings were inauspicious. He was a timid young man who struggled with pettiness. His autobiography tells the stories of his juvenile forays into the realms of deception, his missteps as a young husband, his ambitions to become a gentleman lawyer. It wasn't until he traveled to South Africa to begin work as a corporate lawyer that he encountered those aspects of the world that would sculpt his destiny. Unlike others who would be moved to action by the experience of another person's misery or pain, it was the personal experience of the injustice done to his fellow Indians and other people of color that awakened within Gandhi the will to act.

The first of these experiences took place on a night train from Durban to Pretoria in South Africa. The young, British trained barrister had arrived in the country just weeks earlier to work as a corporate lawyer for an Indian company. As part of his first case, he was sent to Pretoria for a deposition. He was traveling with a first class ticket. In Maritzburg, another passenger entered his compartment, saw that he was a man of color and objected to his traveling in a first class compartment. Two officials of the railroad company appeared and ordered Gandhi to move to the third class wagon at the rear of the train. He refused. They threatened him. He remained adamant and was finally carried out of the compartment and placed on the platform. There he stood, shivering in cold mountain air, as the train continued on its way south.

Years later Gandhi was asked by a Christian missionary what he considered to be the most creative experience of his life. Gandhi told him the story of his night in the Maritzburg station.[24] Fischer wrote: "That frigid night at Maritzburg the germ of social protest was born in Gandhi."[25]

It was during the South African years that Gandhi developed the inner qualities that were to become the signature of his outer work. The inept middle-class lawyer metamorphosed into a disciplined spiritual leader and statesman. At the core of his work were two practiced tenets to which he would remain faithful the rest of his life: never use the weakness of another to advance one's own goals; and, secondly, once he had committed himself to fight an injustice, he let nothing dissuade him from continuing that battle. Unless the situation changed. For instance, he set aside the struggle for Indian rights in South Africa to serve in the ambulance corps during the Zulu rebellion. A changed situation called for a changed response. Like Steiner, he worked out of the realities of the situation, the context in which he found himself.

Similarly, at the height of the battle with General Smuts, on the eve of a mass march to demonstrate against the South African government's refusal to grant Indians certain basic human rights, Gandhi was notified of a railroad strike by the white workers. Louis Fischer writes: "Gandhi immediately called off his march. It was not part of the tactics of Satyagraha, he explained, to destroy, hurt, humble, or embitter the adversary, or to win a victory by weakening him. Civil resisters hope, by sincerity, chivalry, and self-suffering, to convince the opponent's brain and conquer his heart."[26] General Smuts wrote about his experience with Gandhi in a memorial edition of essays celebrating Gandhi's 70th birthday: "It was my fate to be the antagonist of a man for whom even then I had the highest respect.... He never forgot the human background of the situation, never lost his temper or succumbed to hate, and preserved his gentle humor even in the most trying situations."[27] Yet at the same time, he admitted that the negotiations with Gandhi were trying. Gandhi deliberately broke the laws he believed infringed on the humanity of the Indians and called upon others to do so also; Smuts was obliged to uphold those laws. Their respective obligations placed them inescapably in confrontation with one another.

Throughout their confrontations and negotiations, neither lost his respect for the other, nor did either of them shirk from doing what he thought was right.

—

In *The Philosophy of Freedom*, written many years before the beginning of the Waldorf school, Rudolf Steiner characterized this quality of social relationship: "To live in love of the action, and to let live in the understanding of the other's will, is the fundamental maxim of the free individual.... The free individual lives in confidence that what is free in oneself and what is free in the other belong to one spiritual world, and that their intentions will harmonize. Free individuals do not demand agreement from their fellow human beings, but expect to find it because it is inherent in human nature. I am not referring here to the necessity for this or that institution, but to the disposition, the attitude of soul, through which one, aware of oneself among one's fellow human beings, most clearly expresses the ideal of human dignity."[28]

Collaborative forms of self-governance are only possible if we embrace this ideal of individual freedom that comes so clearly to expression in Gandhi's life and work. By doing so, we can return the idea of governance to its original meaning: the forms we give ourselves to guide us in fulfilling what we have set out to accomplish.

6

A Culture of Collaboration

Collaboration has become one of the most often used terms in modern organizations. Like many other words that have become ubiquitous in contemporary culture, this overuse has robbed it of any clear meaning. As a word, it is empty; as a practice, most necessary. We face the question: Can we move our understanding of collaboration out of the empty ambiguity of our time into a space of experienced practice? We must think of collaboration as a verb.

It was originally a verb — *co(n)* meaning "with," and *laborare* meaning to work, to work with, to work together. Was it used in ancient Rome? Doubtful. According to the Oxford dictionary, it appears relatively recently, in nineteenth-century France. The first noted use is in 1801 to describe a person who practiced collaboration; at this point in history, in a positive sense. From the beginning it was used in the context of cultural activities—the writing of a play, the writing of a novel, scientific research. Collaboration is a specific form of working together—the working together of human beings, who bring something new into the spiritual/cultural life of their time.

In this sense, collaboration is quite different than simply doing things together or helping one another get things done.

It describes a quality of interaction between two or more individuals through which they are able to bring something new into existence. I used to live and teach at a farm-based school in Vermont. Our neighbors were also farmers. We used to get together to help one another bring in the hay. These haying "bees" were lively affairs, full of camaraderie and laughter, with children, wives and workers in an egalitarian mix out in the fields. They were extremely enjoyable, an impromptu celebration of neighborliness, possible only through the proximity of our properties and the fact that in some way we were all farmers. And although we all enjoyed them, and I think, in a way looked forward to them, they didn't lead to anything other than helping one another get the hay in. Charlie went on being the same gruff, unpleasant person he had always been; Arvid never stopped looking at us with Finnish amusement. And we all knew Matt thought of us as cheap labor.

I had a similar yet different experience when living in a traditional Mennonite community in Virginia. There various kinds of "bees" were an integral part of the fabric of community life. People would get together to plant, to harvest, to can, to quilt and sew, to slaughter, to build—almost every aspect of a farmer's life was shared among neighbors. These people worked together and enjoyed it. Through generations of practice, they had raised working together to an art. There were no committees to organize things, no guidebooks with carefully programed processes, no assessment forms. They worked together. And through their working together, they not only got things done, but also wove the threads of community, a community that had existed before they had been born and would continue after they died. Although I was still quite young and skeptical at the time I was able to share in their lives, I slowly began to recognize that the community within which they lived and worked and worshipped was something much more than simply living close together and doing things together. It was a living reality within which each individual found the strength, support and guidance to be a good person. They helped each other practice goodness. Over the time I spent there, I found a feeling of responsibility for this quality also grow within me—for the shared values and culture of these very wonderful people .

The working together of the Mennonites is qualitatively different than the loose neighborly work "bees" of my Vermont years. The communal fabric is fundamentally religious; the individuals participating do so out of a deep commitment to a common faith. What they do together is in service to this community of faith. Here there is a shared spiritual striving that raises their common efforts beyond being good neighbors.

This, I believe, brings us closer to what we intuitively hope for when we think of collaboration. Working together within the context of a traditional, religious context is rooted in humanity's past. Working together to envision and craft new spiritual/cultural contexts is the key to humanity's future. Collaboration is the way of meeting this challenge.

During a recent colloquium hosted by the Center for Contextual Studies[29] on teaching and learning, I was given the opportunity to speak about collaboration and to explore the circumstances and conditions under which a successful collaboration can take place. It was an exploration of the various aspects of a collaborative context. The thoughts shared with the participants during that colloquium form the core of this chapter. Since the colloquium was focused on education and the relationship between the teaching learner and the learning teacher, much of what is put forward here is specific to, although not necessarily limited to, an educational context.

Education is the focal point of a paradigmatic cultural watershed. For hundreds of years, the role of education has been to impart to children the knowledge and character traits they need to fit into and play a role in an existing socio-cultural setting. This is still the fundamental assumption behind most educational policy. There is the tendency to believe that the future will emerge in a linear fashion out of the past; that past practice will be the basis for future developments.

There are many indications that we have reached a juncture in human development where these assumptions no longer hold true. The context within which children grow and learn is changing too quickly and too radically. The traditional educational approaches can no longer provide children with the kind of guidance and support they need to find a healthy relationship to the world around them. The challenges we face demand fundamentally, not incrementally, different approaches. As educators, we find ourselves confronted with the challenge of creating learning environments within which children can attain, refine and strengthen the skills they will need in this fundamentally changed world. Education is no longer a matter of instructing children and instilling in them the skills and knowledge they need, but rather of awakening in children the capacities they will need to respond creatively to the changing world around them. This shift in focus permeates all of education, what happens in the classroom as well as the social climate of the culture surrounding the classroom; the quality of the relationship between teacher and student, but also among faculty members and between faculty members and families.

We are facing a cultural shift, not a curricular shift. It is a question of how, not what.

The Partnership for 21st Century Skills[30] has worked with teachers, parents, social scientists and business interests to come up with a list of what they call "21ˢᵗ century skills." Topping the list are what have come to be known a the "4 Cs": creativity, critical thinking, communication and collaboration. These are not intended to replace the meat and potatoes of American education—the basic academic skills, the 3 Rs—but to inform the socio-cultural context within which they are taught. Reading, for example, should be taught in such a way that students exercise the "4 Cs" as they learn to read. A great deal of literature has become available in recent years concerning how this might be done; the abundance of how-to guides is almost frightening: a new book or manual on collaborative teaching techniques is published every day.

This flurry of interest does reflect a growing recognition that the values practiced in the learning environment have a direct effect on learning itself. Education takes place within a cultural context. School culture plays an equally important role in student learning as curricular content or content delivery techniques. Some of the most in-depth recent research of school culture has been done by a team headed by Dr. Kent Peterson, professor in the Department of Educational Administration at the University of Wisconsin-Madison and Terry Deal, professor at the Rossier School of Education, University of Southern California. They have defined school culture as an underlying "set of norms, values, beliefs, rituals and traditions that make up the unwritten rules of how to think, feel and act".[31] It provides the emotive medium in which the various aspects of school life find their meaning, or, in the lack of a coherent culture, fail to do so. In the latter case, Peterson and Deal speak of "cultural toxicity" and venture to say that this is one of the primary reasons schools fail.

The culture of a healthy school will reflect a "widely shared sense of purpose and values that is consistent and shared" among staff members, "group norms of continuous learning and school improvement," "a sense of responsibility for a student's learning," "collaborative and collegial relationships," and "a real focus on professional development, staff reflection and sharing of professional practice."[32] Teachers will have a common understanding of their goals and how to achieve them; they realize that this is an ongoing developmental process which engages everyone involved; they are carried by an inner sense of the responsibility they bear in student learning; they understand that their working relationships with one another and the students is the key to achieving what they strive for; they work at getting better at what they do and how they do it with one another.

These shared understandings, values and practices come to expression in the metaphors and stories, through which school life is passed on, the rituals, the songs, the celebrations, etc. In a healthy organization, there will be a high degree of congruence between what the school says is important and what actually lives there.

Although we need to keep in mind that their vision of a successful school is limited in ways that a Waldorf perspective does not have to be, Peterson and Deal see collaboration and collegiality as playing a primary role in nurturing healthy school culture.

There are, however, different levels of collaboration. The simplest form of collaboration lies in the sharing of questions, problems, and solutions among teachers with similar subjects or age groups. These exchanges revolve around sharing teachers' experience, what has worked or not worked. They provide a wonderful opportunity to pass on what has been gleaned and acquired over the years.

A second level of collaboration becomes apparent when a group of teachers face a challenge that none of them has faced before. In this situation, they must share their experience, step past it, and attempt to discern an appropriate response. This is different than merely sharing ideas and experience. Here experience becomes a tool to understand something new, not a tried and true response to a recurring situation.

These first two levels of collaboration are driven primarily by outer circumstances. The next levels find their impetus from within. Together they form what Deal and Peterson term a "shared collaborative." These are collaborations driven by inner questions. They have their source in two things: the inner striving to become a better teacher, and the desire to gain deeper insight into the nature of the developing child and young person. They come to practical expression in the development of curricula, collaborative teaching, new forms of student intervention, and so forth.

There is an inner shift that takes place between those collaborations that are sparked from outside and those that come from within. Take for example the challenge of mobile web devices. Ten years ago, they were practically unknown; today they are ubiquitous. At first glance, they fit into what is described above as a second level collaboration: a new phenomenon to be met creatively. Schools approaching the question from this point of view usually come to some variation of two basic approaches. Either they ban or limit their use, or they embrace them as an exciting new technological advance and re-design curricula around the virtual world of information they make readily accessible.

One can, however, raise the question to another level. Why do students often seem to find the virtual world more interesting, more enthralling than the real world? How does the relative ease of information acquisition and the illusory interpersonal connectivity facilitated by the Web change young people's relationship to the immediate world around them, the immediate social context, and, finally, to their own selves? What effect does the virtual world of digital reality have on the incarnating individual? The in-depth exploration of such questions can lead to the questioning of our basic assumptions concerning the nature of education and open possibilities for educational approaches that are better able to meet the real developmental needs of children today. At this level of collaboration, a faculty becomes a collaborative research team able to forge new paths in education through shared insights into the true nature of children's' learning. The school, both as a cultural entity and an educational setting, becomes an intentional space able to shape itself to the genuine soul-spiritual needs of the child in the present.

Such shared exploration opens to a further dimension of collaborative encounter. The shared striving to better understand the learning child, that is the child in the process of becoming, leads us from sharing what we know about children into a shared relationship with the children, in which we struggle to hear what it is they have to say to us. This relationship is marked by the fact that we do not merely strive to better note what the children have become, but to grasp the reality of their becoming. This entails awakening in ourselves the ability to hear that which is not yet there, but which exists as a spiritual reality in the child. Whether education is to play any genuine role in the future of humanity depends on achieving this level of collaboration among teachers and educators. The future of education lies in the incarnating child, the child in the process of becoming. If we are to be part of insuring that the spiritual aspect of education in this sense be constantly renewed, we must find a level of collaboration that allows us to encounter the spiritual dimension of the incarnating child as well as the spiritual reality of one another.

The first two levels of collaboration described here have to do with what each teacher brings into the school out of his or her past. Developing ways to better share experience and knowledge does much to help the atmosphere in a school. Mentoring programs that accompany the work of a young colleague with interest and support when needed are much more effective than critical reviews.

The third level of collaboration entails an awakening in the present. Teachers cease to see their children as variations on a preconceived developmental model and begin to recognize them as they are. Over the years, I have had the honor and opportunity to facilitate faculty meetings in Waldorf schools in various parts of the world. Whenever a student issue arose, I made it a practice to stop the conversation and take time for colleagues to actually describe the student or students involved. We would strive to create as vivid an inner image as possible. Then we would hear the details of the issue before going on to decide how the faculty would wish to address it. I have also found this approach helpful when working with parents of students.

This intentional step to find the student in the present is, however, not without its consequences. In his autobiography, Rudolf Steiner describes the period in his life when he first became aware of this. Looking back on the events of his thirty-fifth year, the sixty-four year old Steiner writes: "[ ] a profound transformation began in my soul....Knowledge and experience of the spiritual world had always been self-evident to me, whereas to comprehend the sensory world through physical perception caused me tremendous difficulty. It was as if my inner soul experience did not extend far enough into my sense organs to unite fully with what they perceived."[33] He goes on to describe how he began to practice a new quality of attentiveness to what presented itself to him in the sense world. He learned to observe carefully and precisely what was in front of him. He refrained from trying to explain the world through thoughts, and learned to listen to what it had to say to him. He turned this newly acquired and practiced attentiveness towards the people he met. "My skills of observation assumed the task of observing, with complete objectivity and purity, what a person manifests in life. I scrupulously refrained from criticizing the actions of others or allowing affinity or aversion to influence my relationships with them; my whole endeavor was to 'allow human beings, just as they are, to make impressions on me.'"[34] The path Steiner describes is one that leads to a spiritual awakening in the present. His intentional immersion in the sense world allowed him to experience the spiritual reality of this world. "The world is full of riddles. …A riddle arises within the real world as a phenomenon; the solution arises equally in that reality."[35] The awakening of the soul within the tension between knowledge and sensing leads to a new level of knowing, what Steiner termed a "knowing that conforms with reality."[36]

The recognition of this dimension of human consciousness lies at the heart of the higher forms of collaboration—the practiced understanding that the solution to the riddle does not lie in the ability to explain it, but rather in the reality of the riddle itself. At this level, collaboration does not consist of coming up with the best ideas about how to address something, but in finding the path to better understand it. The question is not how much we know about something, but what can we learn from it.

When Steiner first began to speak about education, he spoke of the child as a "sacred riddle": "If we [...] think imaginatively about a child, then, as we face the growing child living into life, we are overcome by the feeling that before us stands a sacred riddle. If we work with the child, we must seek to solve that riddle with a deep sense of reverence. We feel in that growing soul something different from everything we see. We feel that something unknown lives in the developing human being, and that feeling is correct. Our modesty and reverence cannot be great enough when we face the task of educating the child. Our humility before that being who presents us with a new riddle to solve can also not be great enough."[37]

The recognition of this riddle opens the door to a much wider perspective on human development than Western thought is usually willing to entertain. The receptive encounter with the present reality of the concrete, specific child marks a certain threshold. We find ourselves touched by the essential nature of the child's becoming. The answer to the riddle does not lie in what the child has become, but in what the child will become, not in the child's earthly path but in the way the child's spiritual nature brings itself to expression on this path. Only a deeper understanding of reincarnation and karma can guide us as we seek to grasp the solution to the riddle.

At this level of exploration, collaboration ceases to be an organizational practice and becomes a spiritual/cultural reality and thus a source of vitality for an educational community. Such a living collaborative reality comes to expression in a culture of respect, interest, recognition and engagement. The school becomes the living expression of the shared striving to grasp in action the true nature of what Steiner termed "the riddle."

7

Leadership in a Collaborative Setting

One of the biggest misconceptions about leadership is that a leader, due to the vested authority, determines how things are to be done, which goals are to be achieved, and who is to do what in which manner.

Leadership today is a question of listening, not speaking; recognizing, not directing; encouraging, not admonishing. The best leaders willingly choose to follow when the situation arises. They know that questions are more powerful than statements, compassion more powerful than compulsion, and that the shortest distance between two points is only within the narrowest of parameters a straight line. They work with the realities of a given situation and, by doing so, help their colleagues broaden their understanding of it. Good leaders will intentionally work to make themselves superfluous. Personal attachment to any form of an institutional leadership function robs one of the freedom and humility one needs to practice leadership. True leaders reveal themselves through their ability to enable others to take on the responsibilities of leadership.

This is especially true within the context of the social environment we strive to craft in a Waldorf school. It has to do with the spiritual nature of today's educational challenge and appears to be at least part of the reason Rudolf Steiner was leery of any form of statute, especially those which attempted to formalize leadership and decision-making structures. With the evolution of human consciousness, the nature of authority and the individual's relationship to authority change also.

Steiner's antipathy for conventional forms of social organization had its roots in his understanding of the evolution of the human soul. Forms that are appropriate and beneficial for one stage of this evolution would have adverse effects at a later stage. This has taken on a new significance in the current stage—the time of what Steiner termed the consciousness soul—a stage marked by a fundamental shift in how the individual experiences the world around him. The natural instinctive, or intuitive, understanding of one's connectedness with the world and with other human beings is lost and must intentionally be forged anew.

Initially, the conscious soul comes to expression in a sense of separation, of loneliness, even of isolation. The self experiences itself confined within the limitations of what it thinks itself to be. The world becomes an impenetrable riddle. Consider the words of Augustine: "I confess to you, Lord, that I still do not know what time is. Yet I confess too that I do know that I am saying this in time, that I have been talking about time for a long time, and that this long time would not be a long time if it were not for the fact that time has been passing all the while. How can I know this, when I do know what time is, but do not know how to put what I know into words? I am in a sorry state, for I do not even know what I do not know!"[38]

These words, which were written just at the turn of the fifth century, are prophetic. Augustine was far ahead of his time, voicing questions that echo down through the ensuing centuries.

"I am in a sorry state, for I do not even know, what I do not know."

Rudolf Steiner characterized this inner state in a lecture given in Zürich, Switzerland, on October 10, 1916: " [...] what has become and will continue to be the most important characteristic of this time is that people tend to confine themselves within themselves. The consciousness soul expresses itself in this gesture of separating oneself from the rest of humanity, of isolating oneself."[39] This inward movement of the soul is accompanied quite rightly by an experience of isolation. The world becomes a riddle that can only be deciphered by finding a new relationship to other human beings, to the natural world, and to oneself.

For Steiner, any form of social organization that would place obstacles in the path of the individual working to create these new relationships was to be avoided. In the above mentioned lecture, he calls attention to three aspects of this challenge. The first has to do with the problem of personal isolation, the second with dogmatic approaches, and the third with the problem of authority. And he points out that, although the initial expression of the consciousness soul is the loss of a natural or intuitive understanding of and relationship to our surroundings, the further development of the capacities of the consciousness soul, the blossoming of the "soul within the soul," rests upon the intentional development of certain inner capacities: the ability to understand the true nature of human encounters, a spiritually-based independence of thought, and the capacity to form independent judgments.

At this stage of soul evolution, each of us is challenged to acquire the capacities that we often associate with leadership.

This is echoed in the closing remarks of the course that Rudolf Steiner gave three years later for the first Waldorf teachers in Stuttgart:

Permeate yourself with the power of imagining
Have courage for the truth
Sharpen your feeling for responsibility of soul."[40]

He expected each teacher to awaken the capacities for leadership within, which today include the ability to recognize the leadership of another. In a modern collaborative culture, leadership and followership go hand in hand.

The codification of authority, any form of statute that defines relationships within the social context has the tendency to dull an individual's awareness of the living dynamics of the social organism, of which one is an integral part. The primary danger of any form of institutionalization today is that people tend to fall asleep. The path of institutionalization is one of increasing drowsiness, the dulling down of individual interest, the strangling of initiative. As long as someone else is responsible, I don't need to worry. I can find my niche and stay safely hidden away. The lack of individual engagement makes forms of leadership and authority necessary that no longer correspond to the inner necessities of human life.

As we proceed into the 21st century, the proving ground of the consciousness soul, we are desperately in need of a new concept of leadership, not an incrementally adjusted concept that merely takes into account the popular notions of a well-fed consumer society, but a fundamentally different approach, which nurtures engagement, interest, a sense of responsibility, the willingness to look beyond the narrow scope of one's own interests. Above all, it must be concrete, a real response to social challenges of today.

When Robert Greenleaf first published his thoughts on servant leadership, he described his inner path to come to grips with this changing reality.[41] Max DePree does something similar in his slender gem of a book *Leadership Is an Art.*[42] Their words ring true; they reflect a lived reality. Both of them describe the inner striving to live up to the demands of what is essentially a covenantal relationship; neither takes his position for granted. Those interested in a deeper understanding of the fundamental change in the role of leadership that we face today will ignore the terminology and focus their attention on the nature of their striving. The words themselves mean nothing.

Leadership today is a contextual reality. It has less to do with the individual "leader" than with the consciously shared intentions of a group of individuals striving to met a common challenge. Within this circle, leadership will emerge depending on the specific nature of the task at hand. In a moment of collegial crisis in one school with which I was involved, the receptionist brought qualities of imaginative social action into the situation that led the school towards a creative solution. During a heated discussion among co-workers at a residential social therapy community concerning future development of the facilities, the gentle observations of one quiet individual, a house mother, opened the discussion to a previously unvoiced dimension of the question. Her perspective led the group to a new level of dialogue.

The story of the "lost expedition," Ernest Shackleton's failed attempt to cross Antarctica, offers insight into the kind of paradigmatic shift I believe we are facing. On August 1, 1918, a day when the consciousness of most Europeans was held captive by the declaration of war, a small ship set sail from Liverpool across the Atlantic. Its destination was Antarctica and its journey had nothing to do with the cataclysm that was about to leave an indelible mark on European civilization. It was not a warship, but a research vessel bound for the last great frontier on the planet. The leader of the expedition was a man named Ernest Shackleton. The fate of the *Endurance* and the journey of the 28 men that made up Shackleton's team is a story of extraordinary courage that illuminates the qualities of leadership and collaboration that make truly great social endeavors possible.

—

The Story of the Lost Expedition

The voyage of the *Endurance* began at the height of summer in the Northern Hemisphere. As the northern summer turned to fall, the ship sailed south into the Antarctic spring. The plan was to navigate through the summer ice with the goal of reaching the Antarctic continent before the ice began once again to form the impregnable winter pack ice. The journey began well: crossing the Atlantic to Brazil, where Shackleton joined the ship was without incident. After stocking up, the ship followed the coast of South America before entering into the great southern ocean. Its last landfall was South Georgia Island, a bleak mountainous outpost with a small harbor used primarily by whalers. From there the ship continued southward towards the great ice pack that surrounded the continent of Antarctica.

Just two days after leaving South Georgia Island on December 7, the *Endurance* met pack ice much farther north than anyone had expected. The voyage became increasingly difficult as the ship had to pick its way through the ice, constantly in search of open water. By New Year's Day, they had only progressed about 500 miles and found themselves up against thick pack ice. Days were spent making their way along the edge of the pack, looking for a way in. By the end of the month, the ship was frozen into and drifting with the pack. For another month, the crew worked to break the young ice around the ship, hoping that the floes would open up and let them reach open water, but by the middle of February, it had become clear that the brief Antarctic summer had passed: their only hope was to wait for spring to open the ice.

Throughout the winter, the ship remained locked in the ice, moving with the great frozen masses as they drifted with the winds and currents. The expedition settled into a routine of work, research and play. Temperatures well below zero became the norm, daylight disappeared. The long cold months were relieved with song and stories, celebrations and skits. All looked towards the spring with hope that their voyage could continue as planned.

The events that changed a courageous journey of exploration into a heroic tale of leadership and collaboration began when the ice began to break up in late September 1915. For months now the crew had been cut off from all contact with the world they had left behind. WWI was raging, they were believed lost. The *Endurance* was caught between three great ice floes. As the young ice melted, the aged floes began to move, grinding against one another, being lifted up and crashing down. The forces at work were gigantic and too much for the *Endurance* to bear. Powerless to do anything to save her, the crew was forced to stand by and watch her demise.

Her end came in late October. For days, the men had salvaged as much as they could from the ship, lugging it over the ice to their camp on one of the larger adjacent floes. October 27 was the last day the crew spent on board ship. Shackleton wrote: "After long months of ceaseless anxiety and strain, after times when hope beat high and times when the outlook was black indeed, the end of the *Endurance* has come. But though we have been compelled to abandon the ship, which is crushed beyond all hope of ever being righted, we are alive and well, and we have stores and equipment for the task that lies before us. The task is to reach land with all the members of the expedition. It is hard to write what I feel."[43]

The *Endurance* had been locked in the ice a total of 281 days and had drifted more than 570 miles with the pack. When the time came to abandon her, she was 346 miles from the nearest land, a small island where there was a hut with emergency rations left by an earlier Swedish expedition. That night Shackleton called the crew together thanked them for their steadiness and morale and told them that he intended to try and cross the ice to reach Paulet Island. They ate dinner together and turned in, sleeping in the tents that would be their homes for the coming months.

"For myself, I could not sleep. The destruction and abandonment of the ship was no sudden shock. The disaster had been looming ahead for many months, and I had studied my plans for all contingencies a hundred times. But the thoughts that came to me as I walked up and down in the darkness were not particularly cheerful. The task now was to secure the safety of the party, and to that I must bend my energies and mental power and apply every bit of knowledge that experience of the Antarctic has given me. The task was likely to be long and strenuous, and an ordered mind and a clear programme were essential if we were to come through without loss of life. A man must shape himself to a new mark directly the old one goes to ground."[44]

Shackleton and his men began their journey across the ice three days later, abandoning everything no longer needed. They took with them two boats, which fully loaded with gear weighed more than a ton apiece. Placed on specially built sledges, the men pulled these along hastily built pathways while the dogs pulled the sleds with rations and cooking gear.

I have tried many times to imagine this moment of breaking camp and setting off over the ice. The ice was not flat. The landscape was surreal, with great heaps of ice pushed up against and on top of each other. Over 300 miles away was a barren island, inhabited only by seals and birds. This was their goal. Everything needed to sustain them on this journey, including the boats, which would become necessary when the ice broke up, had to be carried or pulled along. The ship, which had given them a sense of home, a place of security in the midst of this unfriendly landscape with its stark beauty and violent storms, lay crushed behind them, shattered by the forces at work in the shifting floes over which they would have to travel. The accounts say that no man lingered or lost courage, but each cheerfully put himself to the task at hand. Together they broke camp, together they shouldered their burdens, together they set out to cross the uncertain ice.

Ernst Shackleton was formally the commander of the expedition. He was familiarly known among the men as "Boss." He took the responsibility of this position very seriously.

"There were twenty-eight men on our floating piece of ice, which was steadily dwindling under the influence of wind, weather, charging floes, and heavy swell. I confess that I felt the burden of responsibility sit heavily on my shoulders; but, on the other hand, I was stimulated and cheered by the attitude of the men. Loneliness is the penalty of leadership, but the man who has to make the decisions is assisted greatly if he feels that there is no uncertainty in the minds of those who follow him, and that his orders will be carried out confidently and in expectation of success."[45]

He perceived his leadership role in the expedition, however, as a function rather than an honor. He did more and took less than those entrusted to his care. He never asked anyone to do something he was not prepared to do himself. Major decisions were openly discussed; every voice was heard. From the moment they were forced to abandon the *Endurance*, the only challenge was to get everyone back safely. They had failed to achieve the original goal of the expedition to cross Antarctica by foot. There would be no acclamation, no honor of discovery. The carefully planned routes and safeguards were now no more than ashes in the wind. The entire dynamic of the group shifted. Everyone gave their best to ensure that no member of their company would have to be left behind. They achieved this by using all their combined skills to live in dialogue with the real conditions surrounding them. In a way, they helped one another become at one with the reality of their surroundings. Although each one was expected to and did look out for himself, each man also remained aware of the other.

There is much that can be learned from the life of these colleagues as they drifted through the frozen Antarctic waters on a shrinking piece of ice, enduring temperatures that rarely rose above freezing. Humor and games were essential, small variations in the daily rhythms alleviated the deadening dullness, tasks were rotated, essential functions were taken on by those who could do them best.

Those men who took on positions of responsibility were not rewarded for doing so; they were asked to sacrifice more. The egalitarian communality of their lives together made it possible for them to recognize freely and celebrate the capacities and skills of one another.

As the months passed, their circumstances grew increasingly dire. Anyone aspiring to leadership should read the accounts carefully. Imprisoned on their floe by fields of impassable, half-frozen ice, they passed within 60 miles of Paulet Island. The next land was another 100 miles to the north. As the pack continued to drift northward, the ice began to break up. Gaps of open water appeared. Floes crashed against one another, killer whales broke surface in the openings. The floe upon which the expedition was camped melted and shrank. The danger grew that it would break apart as it rose and fell upon the waves. Finally they abandoned this last vestige of solid footing and took to the boats for a harrowing journey between the unpredictable floes.

When they finally reached land, it was nothing more than a strip of barren sloping stone between the raging sea and the glacier covered cliffs of Elephant Island. Although they once again had solid earth beneath their feet, they were completely at the mercy of the elements.

The Antarctic summer was at its end. Weakened as they were from the exertions of the journey and the lack of food, Shackleton was certain that they could not survive another winter on the ice. Choosing five companions, he readied the most seaworthy of the three open boats and set off across 800 miles of open water to find help. By the time they reached the western shore of South Georgia Island sixteen days later, they didn't have the strength to pull their boat from the water. Two of the men were so weakened that they could barely walk. Of the four remaining, one stayed behind to care for his two comrades, while Shackleton, Worsely, and Crean set out to cross the mountains to the whaling harbor on the eastern shore.

According to their rough map, the distance across the island to the whaling station was only seventeen miles as the crow flies. The interior of the island was unexplored and believed by the whalers to be inaccessible. Between Haakon Bay, where Shackleton's crew had landed, and Stromness, where they could count on finding help, were rocky, snow-covered peaks rising some 9,000 feet above the sea.

They traveled light, taking only a rucksack with proviant for three days, a Primus lamp, a small cooker, a 50' length of rope and a carpenter's adze to use as an ice axe. Their clothes were in tatters, they had put screws through the soles of their boots for traction. Leaving at 2:00 AM on the morning of May 19, 1916, they climbed up into the interior highlands and set off, skirting the high peaks, for the other end of the island. More than once they found themselves at the top of a ridge or the bottom of a slope with no way to proceed and had to retrace their steps and try again. They stopped only to rest briefly and eat something, then continued on, traveling through the night by the light of a full moon. The final descent was by rope in the stream of a 30' waterfall. Shackleton wrote about this moment:

"At the bottom of the fall we were able to stand again on dry land. The rope could not be recovered. We had flung down the adze from the top of the falls and also the logbook and the cooker wrapped in one of our blouses.

That was all, except our wet clothes, that we had brought out of the Antarctic, which we had entered a year and a half before with a well-found ship, full equipment, and high hopes. That was all of tangible things; but in memories we were rich. We had pierced the veneer of outside things. We had 'suffered, starved, and triumphed, groveled down yet grasped at glory, grown bigger in the bigness of the whole'. We had seen God in his splendours, heard the text that Nature renders. We had reached the naked soul of man."[46]

After reaching the settlement, they lost no time before rallying the help they would need to rescue the rest of the crew. The three men left in Haakon Bay were picked up by one of the Norwegian whaling vessels and arrived in Stromness on Monday afternoon. The 22 men who had remained on Elephant Island were rescued on the fourth attempt on August 30, 1916. They were packed and ready to go when the Chilean steamer appeared in the harbor. No-one had doubted that Shackleton would return for them.

"When I look back at those days, I have no doubt that Providence guided us, not only across those snowfields, but across the storm-white sea that separated Elephant Island from our landing place on South Georgia. I know that during that long and racking march of thirty-six hours over the unnamed mountains and glaciers of South Georgia it seemed to me often that we were four, not three. I said nothing to my companions on the point, but afterwards Worsley said to me, 'Boss, I had a curious feeling on the march that there was another person with us.' Crean confessed to the same idea. One feels the 'dearth of human words, the roughness of mortal speech' in trying to describe things intangible, but a record of our journeys would be incomplete without a reference to a subject very near to our hearts."[47]

———

There has been a good deal written about Shackleton in recent years. A number of authors have analyzed his leadership skills, listing the attributes and practices that made him an exceptional "leader." There is a great deal to be learned from these studies. What they do not, however, bring to light is the paradigmatic, or fundamental, shift in the nature of human relationships that the Shackleton expedition represents. This last great expedition of the "heroic age of exploration" was one of the first great deeds of a new age of human relationships. It marks the shift from a culture of leaders and followers, to one of leadership and the recognition of the part that individual responsibility and understanding play in the success of the whole.

This culture of leadership is also essential within a school community. Imagine that once a week you have the opportunity to enter into a lively, focused dialogue on the future of education. Your partners in this endeavor are your colleagues, the conversation centers around children you all know, on moments taken from the teaching experience of one or more of your colleagues or on ideas that someone is thinking about trying in his or her classroom. The conversations are lively and spirited. At times, they even lead to heated differences. Pedagogical questions arise that lead you back to a closer consideration of Steiner's thoughts. What did he see as a possibility, or how did he see the situation?

These meetings are held in a mood of joyful, enthusiastic professionalism. Excitement at the possibility of better understanding the path of the incarnating child, the nature of imagination, or the signature of the I in the will gives the gathering a quality of almost religious anticipation. Interest is high. "I wonder what he'll have to say about Betsy's poem?"

The time flies. One is always somewhat disappointed when it comes to an end. Colleagues leave refreshed, there is a pleasant hum of conversation as the group disperses. Everyone senses that what lives in these meetings flows on into the classrooms, a stream of warmth and light that weaves a sense of unity and purpose into the striving of all who come to the school. One feels that something real has taken place.

These meetings provide a sense of direction. Everyone recognizes that what develops in them will lead in the right direction.

A growing number of teachers have become aware of the importance of an ongoing pedagogical dialogue and the role it plays in providing a school community with a sense of leadership. Yet most of them have trouble reconciling the quality of collegial encounter sketched out above with their own experience of faculty meetings. These often seem to be the antithesis of what one would hope for. Instead of lively, creative pedagogical exploration in which the future of education begins to take shape, one finds oneself confronted with rigid agendas, the endless minutiae of daily business, poorly structured presentations, reports, and so forth. One leaves feeling as though one had been put through the proverbial wringer.

In such meetings, the level of conversation rarely transcends the personal and often becomes entangled in the thickets of opinion and interpretation. Those with the gift of facilitation smooth the waves of conflict with artful compromise. Confrontation is avoided at all cost. A monotonous harmony becomes the goal, a goal that always seems just beyond one's grasp. No one speaks too openly for fear of upsetting the applecart, of disturbing the peace. One can feel everything grind to a standstill.

Those who try to voice the problem find that their voices cannot be heard, and soon they cease to speak or they just disappear. Rarely do the meetings approach the mystery of, as Shackleton wrote, "the naked soul of man"; rarely can one say with Worsley: "Boss, I had a curious feeling on the march that there was another person with us."

The vitality of the pedagogical dialogue is directly connected to what seems to be most missing in schools today: leadership. The lack of leadership comes to expression in many ways. Institutionally, it becomes apparent in the growing presence of bureaucracy, tendencies towards top-down administrative structures, growing disparities between what a school says about itself and what in fact lives in and between the classrooms, and in the codification of relationships. Rules and regulations replace direct encounters. Teachers begin to become more invested in their lives and activities outside of school than in the life of the school itself. An atmosphere of disengagement begins to pervade everything.

This creeping disengagement exacerbates the innate tendency in any institution towards rigidity in its policies and procedures. Those charged with ensuring the continued existence of the institution find themselves faced with having to enforce compliance. For example, in one school I have worked with, they had taken to docking teachers' pay in cases where the teacher was not living up to contractual expectations (attendance at faculty meetings, timeliness in submitting reports, and so forth). Increasingly coercive measures have, in turn, a detrimental effect on the quality of interaction between teachers, and between teachers and parents. Although colleagues may not stint in the time and effort they invest in their teaching, they do begin to feel that the "school" is but a place to work, and they begin to resent the pressure to participate in anything related to the life of the school as a whole. Parents often become more aware of what they perceive as the school's deficiencies than its strengths. Questions that could be the basis for a productive dialogue instead tend to escalate into conflicts; varying points of view lead to the formation of fronts within the school community.

Over time, the collaborative ideal becomes a reality of isolation. In this situation many schools are tempted to turn to the very form that Steiner strove to overcome as he worked towards the founding of the first Waldorf school in Stuttgart 1919. Leading up to the founding, and then later in talks about the work of the Waldorf school, he articulated a new form of pedagogical leadership. The approach he described broke radically with what was ubiquitous at the time, and, still today, challenges us to re-think the way we conceive of institutional governance especially in the field of education.

At the heart of Steiner's vision we find the dynamic pedagogical dialogue described above: the ongoing collaborative striving to better understand the developmental signature of the growing child. This evolving understanding would be the source of pedagogical inspiration, the well-spring out of which a new educational impulse would gradually take form. He spoke of this in a number of different ways. The first time was on the evening before the beginning of the two-week preparatory seminar for the first faculty members. In that setting, he spoke of the need for each teacher to take full responsibility for the school. This was only possible if they could engage themselves fully. Thus there would be no headmaster, principal, or other external unifying instance. The sense of unity that would provide them with a shared center was the ongoing work with what Steiner would bring in the coming days: "If we work hard this seminar will engender in us our spirit of unity."

Although Steiner was clear about the importance of the teachers sharing in the necessary administrative work, it seems that he almost took this for granted. If the teachers were fully engaged in the life and development of the school, they would of course share in the work. But it was the quality of pedagogical dialogue that he would highlight when speaking about the school in the ensuing years. Today this dialogue cannot be limited to the circle of teachers. The socio-cultural changes that have taken place over the last ninety years have created the need for a new sense of partnership between parents and teachers in coming to a shared sense of how best to respond to the developing needs of children.

It appears symptomatic that today, when many schools are struggling anew with questions of governance, leadership, identity and direction, such dialogues have almost completely disappeared.

8

Functional Polarities and Institutional Balance

Some years ago I found myself involved in a school where teachers had, after a good deal of consideration, proposed a recommendation to change the emphasis in the upper grades of the lower school. Over the course of some years, partially under pressure from the high school, partially due to parental pressure, the school had instituted academic skills classes in the middle school years, bringing in specialist teachers to work with the students on math and language skills acquisition. The shift had led to an increase in the number of daily classes, periods had been shortened, and some content that had previously been integrated into the main lesson curriculum was moved into the "skills" classes. Both parents and teachers became aware of increasing stress levels among the children. This expressed itself in a number of ways: tiredness and the inability to focus, lack of interest in school, growing number of incidences necessitating disciplinary action, increase in the presence of forms of self-distraction. In response to this, based on their understanding of the developmental learning needs of students at this age, teachers recommended shifting to a program that created longer periods, and increased the amount of time students spent out of doors, working on practical projects, and doing more artistic work.

The response to the proposal when it was presented to the full faculty was symptomatic of a certain dynamic in schools. Although a number of teachers acknowledged the pedagogical attributes of the proposal, this acknowledgment soon disappeared under the weight of objections concerning the institutional implications of such a shift: the number of teaching positions would change, it would be impossible to schedule, parents would never support it, enrollment would drop, if enrollment in the upper grades fell then the high school would not be able to fill its classes, and even if enrollment stayed high the students would not be prepared for the "rigor" of the high school curriculum. Soon counter proposals were being voiced: couldn't we increase the after-school sports program? Maybe the day could be lengthened to increase the length of the periods. Couldn't lunch be shortened?

In the end nothing changed.

It is not the task at the moment to discuss the pedagogical value of either approach. What is interesting, and in many ways tragic, is that this process highlights an innate tension in our schools, one that we rarely recognize and thus are unable to work with creatively.

None of the objections mentioned above were of a pedagogical nature. Each expressed concern that any change in the pedagogical focus, even if it made sense for the students, could have an adverse effect on the institutional realities of the school: enrollment, maintaining the present curricular expectations, current positions, and so forth. There is, of course, some truth in the reaction: any pedagogical change brings institutional change. Institutional change, in turn, affects the lives of the individuals who are involved in the institution. Yet what usually goes unnoticed is the shift in focus, away from the pedagogical reality of the children and towards the perceived or imagined needs of the institution.

The opposite can, however, also be true. A school, as it matures, tends to grow. This growth is accompanied by the addition of new programs, new staff, new facilities, and so forth, all the things a school needs to be a real school. The economic reality of the situation is that a school cannot continue to grow indefinitely. There is a point of balance between growth and the capacity of the community to support the institution. When this point is reached, a school finds itself facing a dilemma. To continue to meet the needs of its students, a school must be able to change and re-focus programs or create new activities and programs. Yet the established programs and the teachers that carry them are part of its institutional identity. In a booming economy, a school may attempt to skirt the issue by continuing to add programs without taking a close look at the established programs and asking whether they continue to serve the needs of the students now in the school. Those concerned with the long-term economic viability of the school must, hopefully sooner rather than later, question the sustainability of the ongoing growth. If we are going to add new programs, don't we have to find appropriate ways to prune back what is already there?

Teachers all too often perceive such a question from members of a Board or the administration as an attack on their pedagogical liberty and respond by defending the established programs from a pedagogical perspective. Such a reaction misses the point. From an institutional perspective, both pruning and growth are necessary aspects of maintaining a healthy, economically viable, sustainable educational environment. The ongoing growth of established programs chokes the possibility of change and initiative. This is an institutional perspective, one innate in the pedagogical mission.

The challenge we face is to create the proper settings to explore such questions from the appropriate perspective.

In many ways the needs of the institution and those of the children are in direct opposition to one another. The former tend always towards what can be repeated and documented, while the encounter with the child is always unique. As institutional structures take over, the tendency to standardize and attempt to replicate children's experience also grows. We begin to speak of "the curriculum," to justify forms of assessment ubiquitous in the mainstream; rules go through a period of inflation; we begin to categorize children, fitting them into the spaces available within the institutional construct; the number of non-teaching positions increases; management structures become necessary to ensure that everything is coordinated: the "school" takes on a life of its own, a life that is often driven by considerations that have little to do with the needs of children.

This innate tension between what we might call the needs of the institution and the unspoken hopes of the incarnating child is the expression of an inner polarity common to every organization. It is present as a constitutive force in the development of any social organism. In a school—a social organism formed around the unfolding individualities of the children—the tension between these two poles can lead to ongoing conflict. If we are able to recognize the role each plays in the life of the school, we can learn to work productively with this tension and craft forms that help to insure the long-term viability of an educational community.

In one of his earliest attempts to share with the public his insights into the intentional inner development of individual spiritual capacities, Rudolf Steiner described these two fundamental poles: "It is true that spirit is more important than the form—which indeed is nothing at all without the spirit—but the spirit would remain idle if it did not create a form for itself."[52] In German, the word translated as "idle" is *tatenlos* meaning "unable to act or take hold of something." Spirit must have form. Within the context of the physical world, spirit must bring itself to expression in physical form; within the context of the etheric world, it must take on living form; in the astral or soul world, the world of relationships, of what lives in the meeting between ensouled beings, it must take on soul form. In this dynamic interaction between spirit and form, we have the entire mystery of life and action, both in nature and in the social settings in which individuals meet, live, and bring their intentions into action.

Spirit and form are by nature polar opposite realities. Steiner describes spirit as pure activity. Form is not activity. Form is form. It always has the tendency to become rigid, inflexible. To remain healthy, the forms we choose to govern ourselves must find the proper balance between the two forces at play in this polarity. They must be forms that are open to constant renewal through the spirit. They must be living forms, able to adapt and evolve in response to the changing needs of the children, parents and teachers involved.

When Steiner began in 1917 to speak about the threefold nature of the social order, he did so within the context of the social tensions threatening to tear Europe apart at that time. He explored the relationships between meso-social institutions (economic, political, educational/cultural) within a macro-social context. Creating the conditions for these institutions to fulfill their intrinsic roles in society would also open the possibility for individuals (micro-social) to participate intentionally in the ongoing transformation of society and contribute to this transformation. He took an open-ended, relational approach to meeting, what was in his mind, the central question of the societal crisis: the social question.

It is important to keep this perspective in mind when you are working with Steiner's ideas concerning social threefolding. He recognized the need for a radical change in how society worked. He was clear that this change could only come from the individuals involved. How this change would express itself at a macro-social level depended on the quality of engagement of the individual in forming relationships within the meso-social.

In other words, the only way to change the world is to work to change the way individuals experience their relationships with one another. Change will come about when individuals begin to act on the insights inherent in this new quality of experience.

Steiner knew from the beginning that the threefold social order had to grow from the bottom up. It was a grass-roots movement. Although he was instrumental in the establishment of the first workers' councils in Bavarian factories, he spoke out against the wish of some functionaries to force the government to pass laws requiring them because they wanted them to be governmental institutions. "In my opinion, if they are introduced in this manner, they will simply become the fifth wheel on the wagon. (This was met with applause from the assembled workers.) The workers' councils must arise out of economic life ... Let the councils form themselves in the different workplaces and don't mess this up with any talk of passing laws; they (the councils) should be there first...".[49] If it were to have a positive influence on the future of human society, no aspect of the threefold social order could be implemented from above.

Rudolf Steiner made no attempt to give the first Waldorf school a "threefold" organizational structure. There were no neat distinctions between the discrete organizing bodies responsible for the three different realms of social activity he had worked so hard to bring to public consciousness in the campaign for social threefolding. The one attempt to make these distinctions statutory in the school's charter dismayed him. Although he did emphasize that only practicing teachers were to have any say in the development of what was taught in the school, his main concern regarding social threefold relationships in the school appears to have been on insuring the independence of the school from outside economic or political pressures. He did not picture the school as an isolated entity, a social organism existing on its own within a greater cultural context; for him the school was an integral part of the greater social context.

In fact, none of the initiatives Rudolf Steiner was involved with had an explicitly "threefold" organizational structure. There were initiatives whose work was rooted in the various realms—economic initiative, political/social initiatives, spiritual/cultural initiatives—but none of these had an internal "threefold" organizational structure. He didn't create structures within the initiatives, some of which were dedicated to questions concerning finance, others dealing with spiritual/cultural concerns, and others dealing with issues concerning rights and responsibilities, contracts and agreements. There was not much time wasted in any of the early endeavors worrying about organizational issues. There was simply too much at stake, too much to be done. The organizational structures arose out of the task at hand and formed themselves around the people actually doing the work.

Does this mean that the perspectives developed by Steiner and his colleagues concerning the three realms of activity within a social organism are of no significance for the development of viable governance structures within an organization? Not at all. If one takes the time to study the way Steiner took up questions belonging to the different realms of activity, both in his work with the Anthroposophical Society and with the initiatives that grew out of his work, it becomes apparent that he distinguished between them in the way he addressed them, rather than by assigning them to different groups or bodies. Economic questions were met with an almost fiery enthusiasm and deep concern for the task at hand; decisions concerning an individual's relationship to an initiative were addressed with frank, open honesty; group decisions were guided with meticulous care for the process. In dealing with economic questions he became the embodiment of brotherly interest illuminated by the attention to practical details; in dealing with questions concerning shared agreements, the guardian of equality and accountability; in addressing questions concerning individual development and the relationship of the individual to an initiative, he modeled freedom, frankness, and respect.

The anthroposophical movement has weakened itself over the years by focusing on trying to understand and apply what Steiner said, rather than following in his footsteps and allowing spiritual insight to manifest itself in action. The challenge of self-governance can be seen as a path towards mastering the ability to respond appropriately when one finds oneself addressing questions belonging to one of the three realms Steiner describes in his work on threefolding. When seen in this light, the structures we choose, the forms we put into place, must be viewed as learning structures or forms designed to scaffold the growth of social competence and sensitivity in these three fundamental areas: competent objectivity in dealing with institutional sustainability, clarity and fairness when addressing the relationship between the individual and the community, participatory engagement in the ongoing quest towards spiritual understanding.

Does Steiner's threefold perspective give the possibility to overcome or transcend the polarity described at the beginning of this chapter? Perhaps. In an evolutionary or developmental sense, form reflects what an organism has become. It is the expression of past becoming.

What is the source of future becoming? This is the developmental pole Steiner refers to in relation to what he calls spirit. Within the context of a school, we find in the established structures, the administrative practices, the programs and curriculum, and the myths and rituals, the traces of what the school has become—the school's institutional identity. If we wish to catch a glimpse of the source of the school's future becoming, we must come to an inner experience of the spiritual activity that strives to bring itself to expression through these forms. The source of this inner experience lies in our encounters with the children and young people we teach. The ongoing dialogue among teachers and between teachers and parents striving to better understand the nature of these encounters and respond to them is the source of the school's ongoing spiritual renewal. It brings itself to expression in institutional growth and change.

Institutional identity and stability are essential to the long-term sustainability of the school as a social organism within the larger social context. We must insure that the available resources, community relationships, and support are cultivated, nurtured, and drawn upon in such a way that the school can serve children for years to come. The pedagogical dialogue is necessary to insure that we are in fact serving the children who seek us out. The vitality and viability of a school depends on both activities, but most especially on the dialogue between the two. It is essential that each informs the other and equally essential that neither defines the activity of the other, for the activity of each realm reflects an essential aspect of a greater whole.

Closer consideration of this dynamic brings to light a third realm of activity in which the two poles meet and overlap. In Rudolf Steiner's work this third realm is described as the judicial or political realm, the realm of rights and responsibilities, contracts and agreements. If we consider it from the point of view of the function it has to fulfill within the social organism, we see that, on the one hand, it has the task of insuring that the acknowledged institutional expectations are being met by those delegated to fulfill them and, on the other hand, that the pedagogical initiatives arising out of the teacher's collaborative deliberations are realized in a manner supportive of ongoing institutional vitality. Through its activity, this middle realm brings the two poles into a dynamic balance. It is the space where the contractual realities of the institution meet the covenantal realities of the pedagogical encounter.

9

Functional Structures

As we know, it is a rare Waldorf school that does not struggle with questions of governance at some point in its biography. Today many schools find themselves in the midst of such struggles. To some extent they revolve around questions of authority, questions which at their worst spiral downward into struggles for power, or they reflect a loyalty to the forms that have been handed down as appropriate for Waldorf schools; in some cases one recognizes in these struggles the inability to create and sustain viable structures out of a sense for the whole. At the center of all of them lies the question as to the identity of Waldorf education.

This question of identity has grown more pressing over the course of the last fifteen years as the number of Waldorf schools has grown and as a new generation of teachers has moved into positions of responsibility within the schools. This has been accompanied by a concerted effort towards institutional stability and assimilation into the greater educational landscape. The push has embraced forms of school development and quality assurance that are ubiquitous in the mainstream, while making efforts to "adapt" them to the special situation of Waldorf education with its focus on individual learning. Although it has resulted in stronger institutional forms and a somewhat more professional "face" for Waldorf education, it has also exacerbated the increasingly existential question: What makes a Waldorf school Waldorf?

The question of identity and that of school governance are inextricably connected. This is what Rudolf Steiner indicated to the teachers of the Waldorf School when they gathered in Stuttgart for the brief but intense training in which Waldorf education was first articulated. Let us look again at the way in which Steiner speaks about the way the school is to be governed. In the following short cryptic passage, he says:

> Therefore we will structure the school not governmentally, but administratively and manage it in a republican manner. In a true teachers' republic, we will not be able to lean back and rest on the directives of a headmaster; we will have to bring to bear what gives each of us the possibility to take full responsibility for what we have to do. Each must be fully responsible.
>
> The role of the headmaster will be replaced by this preparatory seminar in which we will work to acquire the spirit that will unite the school. If we work hard, this seminar will engender in us our spirit of unity.

A careful reading shows that Steiner speaks here about three aspects that are necessary to the school's success. First he speaks about the organizational structure: it is to be administrative, not governmental. Secondly, he points out that the governance model should be republican, not dictatorial. Then he speaks about what it will take to replace the unifying force of the headmaster or principal.

Translated into contemporary language, Steiner is speaking about the three basic functions in an organization: Leadership (the unifying force), management (governance model), and administrative (the way an organization is structured in order to get things done). The later should not be confused with the various administrative functions in schools. These are present in all three areas.

In his book *The Seven Habits of Highly Successful People*, Steven Covey explores two of these three functions and their interdependencies, and points out that although both are necessary, each needs to know its own strengths and weaknesses. Following up on Peter Drucker's remark that "management is doing things right; leadership is doing the right things," Covey develops the picture of a production crew cutting their way through the jungle. "The managers are behind them, sharpening their machetes, writing policy and procedure manuals, holding muscle development programs, bringing in improved technologies, and setting up working schedules and compensation programs for the machete wielders. The leader is the one who climbs the tallest tree, surveys the entire situation and yells, 'Wrong jungle!'"[50]

He then adds: "But how do the busy, efficient producers and managers often respond? 'Shut up. We're making progress.'"[51]

This dynamic is in no way unknown in Waldorf schools and presents one of the most difficult obstacles to all forms of productive change. It reflects a tendency to get so caught up in specific tasks that one loses sight of the bigger picture, the reason or the context of the task in the first place. In schools, this comes to expression in various forms of departmental thinking, in which one can see one's own needs and priorities but is blind to those of others.

If we return to Steiner's vision of a self-governed school, we find that the most fragile and exciting part of his cryptic sketch concerning the running of the school is contained in what he says about the collaborative path to finding a unified center. The shared experience of the "preparatory seminar," if everyone works hard, will serve to "engender in us our spirit of unity." If one stops to consider that neither management nor administration can function without leadership, Steiner's vision of teacher-guided education stands or falls on the question of this collaborative learning experience. Without it, the school lacks a common center, and decision-making becomes a matter either of personal interest with the accompanying tendency towards power struggles or of institutional expediency based on compromise.

The form of self-governance that we are challenged to develop and sustain in the schools hinges on this activity. It manifests itself in pedagogical study, the sharing of teaching and parenting questions and insights and most especially in the ongoing striving to deepen our ability to recognize the spiritual gifts and questions that we encounter in the children. It is a dialogical undertaking, a space in which everyone involved enters into a similar quality of listening and learning with one another as they hope to achieve in the classroom with the children. It is a space of highly focused activity, of a questioning learning, the space in which Waldorf education is constantly being developed anew out of the encounter with the spiritual reality of actual children, the space where Waldorf education comes alive and meets the intuitive forces of the future. It is the only space in which the future of education can be conceived. It has also almost disappeared in a majority of Waldorf schools.

The art of pedagogical study is as important to the health of a Waldorf school as is the art of teaching. This applies not only to what is often narrowly termed "the pedagogical realm." The financial health of our schools is wedded directly to the quality of learning encounter that takes place in the classrooms

—encounters that are enhanced and enlivened through this activity of pedagogical dialogue. The classroom is at once a concert hall and a laboratory, the teacher a participant/observer. Each day, each year should bring insights that allow us to better meet the developmental needs of the children who find their way to us, not merely cater to the supposed wishes of the parents or position ourselves more successfully in the greater educational landscape. Financial health is linked to the evolving vitality of the educational encounter, the verve of learning. And this vitality, this verve, is the spiritual expression of pedagogical collaboration.

When we consider the struggles many schools have today with questions of governance, it seems to make sense not to try to find ways to fix the problem—for instance by importing successful programs or training methods, or hiring consultants to present solutions—but to step back and ask ourselves: Is there a time/space in the school's rhythm that allows this quality of dialogue to unfold? Do we give it the space it deserves? Are the skills necessary for a productive dialogue practiced and cultivated? No form of self-governance can succeed in a school where this dialogue is lacking. Conversely, where it lives, governance takes on a fully new quality. The search for appropriate structures becomes a question of finding forms that allow us to realize the educational impulses that arise out of this intentional, reflected commitment to our children.

Finding structures that work for any given school is no easy matter. There are no general solutions. Each school presents a unique opportunity to develop self-governing structures that serve pedagogical creativity. Although there are no general solutions—the "perfect governance structure" is a contradiction unto itself—there are basic principles at work in every social organism. An understanding of these is helpful.

Due to the nature of their work, schools are social institutions that work explicitly with the future. Although it is clear that as a teacher one often has to deal with the past, learning takes place when a bit of the future lights up in the present. Unlike factories or stores, which deal with the refinement and distribution of materials formed in the past, a school is constantly working with what is in the process of becoming, the manifestation of the evolving individual. It is helpful to keep this in mind: *A school is a working community dedicated to the act of becoming.* When one reads the brochures and websites of many Waldorf schools, one finds language that speaks of education as though it were a product, something that one can deliver—Waldorf being one specific form of educational product. But, education, especially Waldorf education, is by its very nature not a product; it is a hope, a possibility.

It is due to this that we can speak of schools in terms of Rudolf Steiner's thoughts on the threefold nature of the body social as belonging to the spiritual/cultural sphere. If schools were marketing an educational product, they would have to function within the service sector, which is a form of what Steiner speaks of as the economic sphere. A number of educators have recognized this in recent years and have formed for-profit educational services with an explicitly outcome-based approach and very clear learning objectives. These services are run as businesses and, in some cases, have been quite successful. This is clearly not our focus as Waldorf educators and yet in every school we can find a certain tension between those aspects of the school's life that are entwined with the realities of the economic sphere and those that are most closely engaged in the challenge of finding pedagogical insight.

This should be no surprise. Economic thinking, as it has developed in our time, requires outcome-based approaches in order to assess effectiveness. Such approaches must be replicable. When this form of thinking dominates in a school, one finds the tendency towards standardization of both the learning goals and the teaching methods. There is a tendency towards strict forms, repeatable achievements; concern for the outer image presented by the school takes up ever more time and energy. Emphasis is placed on institutional stability, making sure that the school has everything that a school should have; programs mushroom, and the parts start to become more important than the whole.

The tension between institutional stability and pedagogical creativity is an intrinsic reality of every Waldorf school. The challenge of finding appropriate forms of governance can be met only by recognizing that both are essential to the long term existence of a school and by understanding the nature of their relationship in the school as a whole. The striving for institutional stability must serve the cultural-spiritual impulse; the latter cannot be channeled into forms that seem to serve the former. This is what lies behind Steiner's injunction that the vision guiding the development of a school must arise out of the collaborative dialogue of those most intimately connected to the children themselves: the teachers and those parents who choose to see beyond their own child's well-being. Insight into what is needed in education can only come through the reflected encounter with the learning child.

If these two necessary fields of activity in a school are not balanced by a third, one can readily picture the recurring clashes and compromises that must occur in the life of a school. Conflict is inevitable, especially as those who take responsibility for various aspects of a school's life do so with great energy and dedication. The third field of activity is one in which these two polarities find a dynamic balance. Those who are familiar with Steiner's work on questions of social development will recognize that this balancing activity lies between the realms of necessity (economics) and creativity (individual development), and it rests on the agreements, the articulated rights and responsibilities, and on the clearly delineated processes that guide interactions within the community. This is the middle sphere, the "rights" sphere, the sphere in which governance in its narrow sense comes to institutional expression.

Over the course of the last few years, I have come to call these three realms of activity sustainability, accountability, and creativity. Any governance structure adopted by a school must insure time/space and resources for the practice of all three activities and articulate clearly the nature of the relationships between them.

Although a number of schools have worked intensively on developing organizational structures that reflect Steiner's work on the threefold nature of social interaction, there is little or no recognition of the fact that each of these three realms of activity needs to be approached differently in order to be effective.

The archetypal form of a productive pedagogical dialogue is given in what is often termed the "College Imagination"— the words that Rudolf Steiner spoke to the teachers of the first Waldorf school at the beginning of their short, intensive training seminar. In this Imagination, Steiner brings to word the relationship between the task of teaching at this point in the evolution of humanity and the work of the spiritual beings that form the third hierarchy: angels, archangels, and archai. In relation to the concepts strength, courage, light, he shows how these beings inform our work with the qualities of imagination, inspiration and intuition. As one works through the images, one discovers that what is described is a path from the inner work of the individual to the illumination of a community of adults dedicated to children's learning. Each brings internalized experiences into the circle. Through the consciously cultivated connection with the angel, these experiences are raised out of the realm of the personal into a realm where the imaginative reality of what lies behind them can begin to speak. In the circle of colleagues, these individualized experiences flow together with what each colleague brings from the encounters with the children. The archangels bear from one to the other what each has to give, what each has to receive. In this flow of intentional dialogue, the archai bring the light of intuitive understanding.

Whoever has experienced this striving towards insight through dialogue knows that its outcomes cannot be pre-programed. Insight can speak through the words of each and every member of the circle, in a larger sense, through each and every member of the school community. When true insight speaks, through whomsoever is then able to voice it, it unites the circle, and one leaves such a meeting feeling enlivened and strengthened for the work ahead.

The structure of creativity is an open structure, with space for a variety of exchanges, questions, explorations, and challenges. Intent is focused through concrete questions. For instance, in 7th graders, questions having to do with physiological development, learning to read, or how movement supports learning. Perhaps the group studies together. How does Steiner approach the question? What are our observations? The dialogue unfolds step by step, always focused on the goal: to better understand the question in order to let this understanding flow into teaching.

This is a quality of work that has nothing to do directly with decision-making processes, yet plays a decisive role in the development of the school. When done effectively, it creates the spiritual (pedagogical) background against which decisions can become apparent.

Whereas collaborative creativity requires such an open, dynamic structure, the activities of sustainability and accountability require more closed, managed structures. Even these differ, however, from one another. An institution becomes sustainable when all the available resources are stewarded in an ongoing, renewable manner. Over the course of the last several years, there has been a growing awareness that the long-term institutional health of a school rests on a delicate web of relationships. Some of these exist within the institution (personnel questions, human resources in the corporate sense), others in the encounter with the surrounding community (parental relationships, community visibility), and yet others with the society at large (other Waldorf schools, accrediting groups, the global economy, and so forth). In this web of relationships, we find the ecological reality of the school.

Sustainable resource management or stewardship is only possible out of an understanding of the complexities of these relationships. It takes expertise in a number of different fields: finance, law, communication, planning, design, marketing, etc. Any given question must be examined or explored from each point of view. Instead of an open, dynamic dialogue where spiritual or pedagogical insight can arise, we need here a structure that insures the various aspects of any planned initiative can be examined from different points of view.

Pedagogical dialogue provides ongoing renewal of the school's vision in relation to the concrete challenge posed by these children, now. This is what Steiner indicated when he spoke of the unifying force, the dynamic center of an organic whole. Those who take on the challenge of sustainable stewardship accept the task of insuring that the resources and facilities needed to realize this evolving vision are available. Pedagogical dialogue plays a leadership function in the school; sustainable stewardship plays a management role.

The third structural gesture is that of accountability. Questions of accountability appear to take up the most time in faculty meetings and decision-making processes. A lack of clear processes and transparent responsibilities in this realm serves to drain a school of its vitality. Immeasurable amounts of time and individual effort go into finding solutions for problems that arise in this realm. In the process, many of the most sacred aspects of collaborative work are sacrificed—honesty, frankness, consequence, and clarity. What actually is accountability? In the best of worlds, it is what each individual strives for in his or her work. Doing what one has said one would do, fulfilling the responsibilities that are attached to one's position, acting in a manner that reflects the stated goals of the community, the active striving to right whatever wrongs may have occurred in the course of one's work are some facets of this striving.

In creating an accountability structure within a school, we acknowledge consciously the need to help one another live up to these strivings. An accountability structure is also there to insure that what we have decided to do as a community gets done, that there is the needed follow-through on projects, that planning takes place, and that emergent questions are addressed in the proper manner. This is functionally the most selfless of the three realms of activity, yet at the same time it is the most demanding.

The accountability structure stands and mediates between the two poles of sustainability and creativity. It has a balancing function, bringing the activity of each of these realms into a productive relationship with that of the other. This mediating role requires that it be mandated from both sides, from those responsible for the long-term institutional existence of the school and from those who are involved in the daily encounters with the children or young people. Because of this double mandate, the accountability (or realization) structure must take on both leadership and management functions in the life of the school community.[52]

The last fifteen years have seen a mushrooming of administrative positions in schools. Although this is to be expected as institutions pass through their pioneering years and reach a certain level of maturity, it poses a problem. Administration, if not carefully managed, tends to either become bureaucratic or to develop an undue sense of its own importance. Administrative functions are service functions. Good administrative co-workers do not want to be anything else but of service. They are professional service personnel. They expect—with justification—guidance, clear work expectations, and oversight; and they take pride in doing their work well. Anyone in an administrative position who does not find fulfillment within these boundaries is in the wrong position. Any school that hires administrative personnel without giving them proper guidance does them a grave injustice.

The lack of management in the administrative realm is the result of an unfortunate approach to "threefolding" that has spread throughout the school movement, not least due to the establishment of administrative training programs run in conjunction with the recognized teacher training institutes. Placing managerial responsibility for a school in the hands of administrators is somewhat similar to placing financial responsibility for a banking institution in the hands of the bookkeeper. Administration in a Waldorf school serves the realization of pedagogical vision in a sustainable manner. It can be effective in the fulfillment of this task only if it is managed within the framework of the accountability structure that a school adopts. The approach to administrative structures most prevalent in the American Waldorf schools raises administrative functions into the realm of management without insuring that the personnel are adequately trained in the two realms such as management function in this context entails: sustainable organizational development and pedagogical dialogue. In an attempt to rectify this lack, administrators are given responsibility but not authority, the latter being split between a "pedagogical" body and a "legal/financial" body, a practice that leads inevitably to conflict due to the polarity that exists between these two areas of activity. This imbedded conflict potential has been exacerbated to some extent by consultants who work either pedagogically or organizationally, creating what can only be seen as an artificial fragmentation of an organic whole.

In looking back on the first conversation with Rudolf Steiner about the planned Waldorf school, Herbert Hahn closed his recollections with the following remark: "One felt, as he spoke, how the thoughts were set free of the narrow confines of space and brought into a dynamic movement, up and outwards. It became increasingly clear what Rudolf Steiner meant when he spoke of the whole. It was not meant to be an array of parts having no meaning for one another, merely gathered under a common roof. Rather Steiner spoke of organic integrity, a unity in which each part affected and was affected by all the others, and in which everything was supported and held by something greater than the sum of the parts, a transcendent beingness. None of us quite realized that in what appeared to be a sociological exploration of modern economics, Steiner was developing the core gesture of the planned school. This was also to be something other than a mere combination of subjects taught beneath a common roof. With his lively view of an organic whole, he introduced us to an educational method that would live in all the grades."[53]

Careful observation of the dynamics of a school allows us to readily distinguish between these three different fields of activity. Among teachers and between teachers and parents there are ongoing dialogues concerning education. Colleagues will turn to one another to share questions and experiences or to come to a better understanding of a certain child. Parents will come to a teacher to gain insight into their child. Teachers will turn to parents to learn more about a child's life outside of school. These conversations are most fruitful when they lead to insights that empower individual initiative.

Secondly, we have the activity of nurturing economic sustainability: planning, setting financial goals, reviewing progress, building a strong sense of the school in the surrounding communities, managing resources, insuring that the school is able to sustain its institutional responsibilities. This is a very different kind of activity, demanding specific skills and areas of expertise. As discussed above, it forms a polarity to the kind of dynamic dialogue that gives birth to pedagogical initiative. Between the two, balancing one with the other, we have the daily tasks of sending out and paying the bills, writing reports, organizing events, facilitating meetings, supervising staff, overseeing teacher reviews, interviewing job applicants, filing insurance forms, ordering toilet paper, replacing light bulbs, cleaning the bathrooms—everything that keeps the school functioning smoothly.

Each of these activities requires a different organizational structure to be effective. The dynamic nature of pedagogical dialogue in a Waldorf school rests on the individual's interest in and enthusiasm for the anthroposophical educational impulse. From time to time, I still meet with a former colleague, a math teacher. Within minutes of meeting, we find ourselves immersed in an intense exploration of some aspect of Steiner's educational work. I always walk away from these encounters feeling personally enriched, either through new questions or insights. This is the quality of dialogue that gives birth to pedagogical initiative.

Imagine faculty meetings in which a teacher could say, "Could we spend some time today or next week exploring this statement that Steiner made in 1919? I've read it a number of times, and it just doesn't seem to make sense. I'd appreciate your help with it." Or, "Could we spend some time today speaking about Joey in the 4th grade? I have some observations that I hope you can help me better understand." These requests would then spark an informed discussion of pedagogical or developmental issues from which colleagues leave refreshed.

For this to happen a number of things have to be present. First, there needs to be a certain quality of spontaneity based on a true interest in what lives in the other. Secondly, there needs to be a certain level of dialogical discipline. What is speaking? What is listening? How do I contribute to the flow of a conversation? Thirdly, some expertise in the field is necessary. Discussions of quantum physics by individuals who have never gone beyond popular notions of the subject are tedious and remarkably unsatisfying. The same holds true for Waldorf pedagogy. Fourthly, such dialogues depend on the willingness of the participants to venture into the unknown. There is nothing more deadening in a discussion than the statement "Well, in Sacramento we always did it this way." Dogmatism, fundamentalism, being trapped in past experience: these have no place in the dynamic, questioning dialogue.

What is the quality of structure that helps make such dialogues possible? It has to have a certain openness and freedom. There has to be space for everyone to be able to speak; one never knows who at any given point of a dialogue will make the decisive contribution. In fact, insights often come from the most unexpected places. It needs to be a structure of timeliness rather than scheduling. It is similar to the quality of structure found in the learning classroom or in individual meditation, structures which are created in the moment through the intentional focus of the active self. It is a will structure, an artistic structure.

The structure needed to uphold the space of sustainability is quite different. Here the task is not to be constantly opening new vistas of understanding and insight, but to be working out ways to best use the available resources to support the work of the school. This is where the numbers are crunched, program costs analyzed, policies and procedures reviewed, long-range plans developed, and institutional growth measured against these plans. This is in essence a strategic space where decisions are weighed based on their practicability, a pragmatic space in which pedagogical initiative is brought into relationship with the realities of implementation. In the legal structure common to most American Waldorf schools, the Board of Trustees is the steward of this space. It assumes responsibility for overseeing the work of the committees that take up various aspects of the work. Its members practice interest for the life of the school. They become in fact epitomes of institutional interest, carrying the life and the identity of the school out into the surrounding community, while placing their expertise at the service of the institution.

The third structure is that which makes it possible to effectively practice institutional accountability. This must be a highly articulated structure with a clearly mandated coordinating body overseeing and supporting the work of smaller teams responsible for various parts of the school. Here management and pedagogical vision merge to craft the structures needed to get things done and to insure that all involved live up to their responsibilities and agreements.

10

Practical Considerations

The last chapter in this book attempts to address certain practical aspects of a dynamic approach to self-governance. Again the frame of reference is the Waldorf school, but the basic principles and practices are applicable to any cultural organization interested in cultivating an atmosphere of initiative, trust, and engagement among the individuals involved in the organization.

The dynamic approach characterized in the preceding chapters moves the discussion concerning organizational development to a new level. This discussion has so far been focused primarily on the structural aspects of institutional self-governance. Emphasis has been placed on developing structures that enable the institution to fulfill its obligations and complete the necessary tasks in a timely, efficient manner. Many books have been published on the subject, as well as a plethora of manuals.

This primarily structural approach tends to view an organization as the sum of its parts. It strives to bring the various parts into a functional relation to one another and ensure that the various stakeholders are represented in the decision-making processes. Emphasis is placed on allocation of tasks, policies and procedures, process and communication. The tendency is towards highly articulated structures designed to manage the organization and representative bodies or groups designed to insure that each group of stakeholders has a voice. In trying to meet each possible conceived need of the organization, these structures at times become so intricate that most individuals involved in the organization are aware only of the part they play and their own responsibilities and rights within the organization. A picture of the whole and how the various parts interact is held only by a very few.

While such structures may have a refreshing effect in the short-term, in the long-term, they tend to lead to fragmentation and isolation. Individuals are encouraged to focus on their own work and speak up for their own needs. Groups representing the different parts of the organization find themselves vying for time, resources and recognition.

In their work on developmental phases of organizations, Bernhard Lievegoed and Fritz Glasl termed this the phase of differentiation and characterized its primary goal as the creation of a controllable structure whose direction can be easily guided.[54] Although the development of such a structure serves to clarify and objectify the various parts of the organization and their needs and tasks, it tends to lead to a breakdown of human relationships and the loss of a cultural relationship to the spiritual reality of the whole. The step from differentiated organizational structures to a model of dynamic self-governance places the latter in the foreground.

We often turn to tried and true structures to overcome what is clearly one of the most challenging aspects of self-governance: human weakness. Self-governance is always a relative term. The forms we choose must scaffold us as we become increasing capable of self-governance.

I was recently reminded of something I once experienced with a group of 11th graders. Our topic was genetics. We were engaged in a conversation sparked by the question: What does it mean to be human? A number of the students had spoken of people who exemplified their notion of true humaneness: Gandhi, Mother Teresa, Nelson Mandela, Martin Luther King were mentioned. One boy, a young musician who had the infuriating habit of drumming with his fingers on the desk at inappropriate moments, suddenly suggested Miles Davis, the American jazz trumpeter and composer.

In response to my question as to why he was thinking of him the boy replied, "Throughout his life Miles played many different styles of music. But regardless of the style, you can always tell it's him. He played the different styles, but in his own way. Miles was always there. He's like a red thread running through his own life."

There was a moment of silence as the students took this in and pondered it. Then one of the twin girls in the class spoke up. "I don't think you can ever be truly human. You can only be becoming human. If you stop becoming human, you can't be human." Her sister looked at her, and then added, "The only place you can discover a human being becoming is in a real human being."

Self-governance begins with the individual human being, the striving human being, the human being becoming. It is all about finding the becoming human being in the only form this miracle occurs: in ourselves and in one another.

Based on this, we can formulate the first two practical principles of developing a model of dynamic self-governance:

1. Learn to see your school and the school community as a living whole.

2. The self-governing learning culture that Rudolf Steiner envisioned at the inauguration of Waldorf education is centered on the striving individual, the individual becoming.

Balancing these two, often contradictory principles, is the central challenge we face.

Approaching the question of self-governance from an organic, whole-school perspective allows us to re-frame the question and move it to a higher level than that inherent in a structural, differentiated approach. We can begin to understand the different bodies, committees and functions in their relatedness both to each other and the whole. Each entity is validated by the whole; each function finds itself reflected in the whole. The focus shifts away from coordinating the work of discrete bodies to cultivating the dialogue and flow of communication between those groups taking responsibility for specific aspects of the life of the whole school. The work of any specific group is only of as much value as the degree to which it is integrated into the life of the whole social organism.

This holistic approach is intrinsic to Steiner's early work on social threefolding. Each of the three fields of activity is valid in and through its relationship to each of the others. The qualities of polarity and dynamic balance described earlier are essential aspects in coming to a working understanding of the resilient fragility of any living organism.

The dynamic functional balance of the three fields of activity in the social organism can be compared to the increasingly complex physiological balance found between the nervous system, the respiratory/circulatory systems, and the metabolic system in the animal kingdom. They can be found, too, metamorphosed, in the human being. Steiner spoke of this comparative relationship in his first book on the threefold social order, but warned against a direct transference of one to the other: "The present comparison (of the social organism with the human organism) is not an attempt to take some natural scientific truth and transplant it into the social system. Its object is quite different;

namely, to use the human body as an object lesson in training human thought and feeling to a sense of what organic life
requires, and then to apply this perceptive sense to the social
organism. If one simply transfers to the social organism something one thinks one has found out about the human body—as
is commonly done—it merely shows that one is not willing to
acquire the faculties needed for studying the social organism in
the way one has to study a natural organism, that is as a thing by
itself, with special laws of its own."[55]

Although Steiner does differentiate clearly between the
three biological systems and the role each plays in the unfolding of human consciousness, what he stresses when compar-
ing the threefold human organism with the threefold nature
of the social organism is that "there is no such thing as absolute centralization anywhere in the human organism."[56] Each
part is present in every other part, just as the whole comes to
expression in each part. This multi-dimensional interrelated-
ness points "to the existence of a superordinate whole that is
self-organizing and self-transforming."[57] Wholeness is not an
abstraction. The human organism first begins to voice its mys-
teries when one begins to understand the nature of human individuality. The social organism only then begins to make sense
when one begins to understand the role the three fields of activity play in the process of the self-transforming activity of the
individual becoming.

Change and Transformation

The next practical consideration has to do with the nature of
change and the process of change within a community. Honest
self-reflection can call one's attention to aspects of oneself of
which one is not always conscious. From posture to gestures

and mimic, habits and habitual gestures of response to sympa-
thies and antipathies, much of what informs one's daily life is
not illuminated by the light of consciousness. This is also true
in a school community. Anyone who has visited various schools
is aware of this. Although each school may be easily identified
as a Waldorf school, no two feel the same. The atmosphere in
each school is unique. In one school, visitors may be honored
and welcomed, in another ignored. On a visit to one school in
northern Israel, a colleague and myself found ourselves taken in,
as though into a large family, and put to work. One notices how
a school community takes care of its facilities, how time is honored, the noise levels in the classrooms and hallways, the clutter
in the faculty room. Is there a sense of order and beauty? Of
stewardship? Of care? Do people rush by one another or do they
recognize and greet one another? Just as one is usually to a great
extent unaware of the gestures, habits, and tastes that inform
one's encounters with those around, those immersed in the daily
life of a school are usually also unaware of the habit culture in
which they participate and which they perpetuate.

This is also true in the realm of school governance. Some
schools habituate roles and functions even though nobody in
the current faculty is able to fulfill them. Meeting culture per-
petuates itself; colleagues find themselves adopting behaviors
they found objectionable in the beginning of their tenure.
I have known a faculty to rise in force to rally around a colleague who was taken to task for habitually neglecting to meet
deadlines for student reports. Those responsible for insuring
that teachers lived up to their contractual agreements were accused of infringing on the colleague's freedom. Some schools
have so deeply habituated a sense of absolute egalitarianism
that anyone who attempts to take responsibility for giving the
school direction faces ostracism. On the other hand, there are

schools that ritualize engagement and celebrate the movers in the school community. This is different from school to school. A perceptive visitor is often more likely to be aware of the non-reflected currents than are those who are a part of them.

Woven into the cultural habit life are what I have come to term the "unspeakables." These are issues that are known but not spoken, unresolved differences, unvoiced opinions, conflicts that have been buried unresolved, that live on in a school's culture, in its habit life. Take for instance the example of an internationally recognized master Waldorf class teacher whose students regularly are completely overwhelmed in high school because they have not acquired any self-directed learning skills. Or, another, the question of tuition remission for faculty children. In some schools, the teacher's relationship to the work of Rudolf Steiner also belongs in this category. In every school, there are issues "unspoken," which over the years become "unspeakable." If they remain so, they become obstacles to any change in the governance practices.

The step from a structural, differentiated organizational approach to a dynamic, integrative approach is one that requires a transformation not only of the governance structures, but also of the school's habit life. In this sense, such a step can be compared to the steps an individual makes on an intentional path of self-development. Each such step is accompanied by the challenge of overcoming habits and behaviors that place obstacles in the path of one's striving, and strengthening those that allow one to more fully embrace it. Obstructive habits are most effectively overcome by the intentional practice of productive habits. The same holds true in a social context. The only way to acquire the capacities and habits necessary for self-governance are to practice them intentionally. The first phase of any change process of this nature is to create opportunities for individuals to practice capacities of engagement, participation, interest and trust with one another. These capacities become the foundation of a sustainable governance model. It is important to note that they are seldom present at the beginning of the process.

This brings us to a third practical consideration: Any change in the organizational structure must be accompanied by change in the social culture. Change in the social culture arises through the practice of new ways of social interaction. Change can only occur if the people involved want to change, not just to change things.

It is helpful therefore to move from a structural, differentiated governance structure to an integrative, participatory approach in a series of steps or phases. The first phase focuses full responsibility for the entire life of the school in the hands of a very few, trusted individuals. They accept the mandate not only to manage the ongoing operations, but also to facilitate the processes needed to craft a participatory governance model. For the first twelve to eighteen months of the change process, this small group becomes the sole decision-making body in the school. By focusing responsibility, this transition structure creates space for other culture-building activities. It creates the opportunity for teachers, students, staff and parents to engage with one another in new ways and, in doing so, practice new possibilities of engagement. The second phase entails a first step towards decentralization of certain responsibilities and brings a focus on dialogue and communication. Only in a third step is the actual structure delineated and mandates for the three focus areas (sustainability, accountability/realization, pedagogical creativity) drafted. The entire transition process, if all goes well, takes roughly three years.

It is easy to disregard the importance of this transition period. Many colleagues would simply prefer to put a new structure in place and get on with it. They do not recognize the need to become capable of a new form. They do not see that it is they who must change. Institutional change rests on individual change. The transition period allows individuals to practice the kinds of interactions they hope will inform the future of the school community. It is a time to overcome fears and misgivings, to identify and begin to work with the "unspeakables," to explore new pedagogical challenges and possibilities, to initiate new spaces for dialogue: to lay the relational groundwork for a new dynamic in the community, to begin to tell a new story.

This is a period both of creativity and fragility. Care must be taken that the process remains open. The choice of the individuals for the transition team is of the utmost importance. It is best not to choose those who think they ought to be on it for one reason or another. It needs to be a group of people willing to function as a team and to put the health of the process before any personal ideas of how things should be.

Finding the Right Decisions

Change of the nature explored here necessitates the questioning of certain basic assumptions. One of these has to do with how we come to decisions and the role decision-making plays in a self-governing social organism. This brings us to the fourth practical consideration.

In his recently published book *Wille zur Verantwortung* (The Will to Take Responsibility), Valentin Wember writes of the problem posed by collective decision-making, the idea that in a self-governing teaching community, everyone must be included in making decisions. He points out that when addressing the role of decision-making, it is important to keep two things in mind: 1) decisions and, 2) responsibility for the consequences of the decisions. "In an organization two things are bad: To have responsibility without being able to participate in decisions, and to participate in making decisions without having any responsibility."[58] He argues that while the process of coming to a decision is primarily an emotional, intellectual process through which judgments are formed, taking responsibility for the decision involves the will. The total human being is only present when coming to a decision and responsibility for the decision are united in each individual involved. Separating the two leads to a "diffusion of responsibility"; in the end no one feels responsible. Collective decision-making models lead to a lack of individual responsibility.

Wember's analysis of the problem is correct, but, I believe, does not go far enough. To begin to gain a fuller understanding of the nature of decisions and the role they play in an organization, we must address the question: Where do decisions begin?

Most decisions have their source in a question. Without questions, one can simply live with the flow of events, letting things happen as they may. Questions demand of us a more active quality of participation in the world. Responsible leadership today means learning to ask and to recognize the right questions. Questions are the most powerful forces not only in individual development, but also in sustainable organizational change.

For many years I have kept a tiny edition of Rainer Maria Rilke's book *Letters to a Young Poet* on my desk. It accompanied me when we moved from Switzerland to Berlin, from Berlin to California and again from California to upstate New York. It was given to me by a student in a course I gave for young teachers in San Francisco in the early 1990s. I spoke about Rilke's letters one evening; the next day he arrived with a copy of the book for everyone in the course. It was a deed of spontaneous generosity, one of many qualities that would later make this

student a much trusted colleague. On July 16, 1903, Rilke wrote
to the twenty-year-old Franz Xaver Kappus: "You are so young,
so much before all beginning, and I would like to beg you, dear
Sir, as well as I can, to have patience with everything unresolved
in your heart and to try to love the questions themselves as if
they were locked rooms or books written in a foreign language.
Don't search for the answers, which could not be given to you
now, because you would not be able to live them. And the point
is, to live everything. Live the questions now. Perhaps then,
someday far in the future, you will gradually, without even no-
ticing it, live your way into the answer. [...] take whatever comes,
with great trust, and so long it comes out of your will, out of
some need of your innermost self, then take it upon yourself,
and don't hate anything."[59]

There are, of course, all kinds of questions. Not all questions
deserve, require or make possible the kind of inner incubation
and intuitive response that Rilke describes above. "Which way is
the train station?" deserves to be answered: "Continue on down
to the first light, make a left and then your next right." It would
be inappropriate to suggest to a frazzled traveler that he learn to
love his question, to live his question and, at some point in the
future, the world would perhaps provide an answer. One must
learn to differentiate between seminal questions and informa-
tional questions, between the questions one lives with and follows, and those that need answers.

Most all decisions affecting the life of a Waldorf school are
rooted in one way or another in the same soil that gives birth
to the seminal questions. These are the decisions that matter,
the ones that affect the destiny of a colleague, a child, a family, a
class, or even the school itself. These are the decisions that cannot simply be made and implemented, but must be lived. They
are the decisions that, once recognized and acted upon, give

guidance for the more mundane operational and resource management questions. Many schools and other organizations tend to shy away from these decisions and the questions in which they are rooted, and spend unnecessary time disputing subsidiary questions and the decisions related to them. For instance, a faculty may spend hours speaking about the need for and ways to provide support for the fifth grade, but never voice the question as to whether the fifth grade teacher is still the right person to carry the class. The latter question leads towards a different kind of decision than the former. The more time we spend with the former, the less we spend with the latter. Questions and decisions that belong in the same space of engagement as the latter are the ones that are important.

These decisions are not only different in terms of their import. They ask of us that we approach them differently. These decisions live in what we might call the will of the school community. The challenge is to recognize, articulate and affirm them. These are not decisions we "make," implement, and execute; these are to be discerned, affirmed, and lived. Groups mandated with the responsibility for discerning decisions have no power—they serve the evolving needs of the social organism.

Different phases of the decision-finding process require different forms of inclusion. The form of inclusion is determined by the questions posed by the mandated group responsible for the discernment process. Lack of clarity in the questions confuses those who are asked to participate, raising false expectations. These false expectations can be a source of distrust and lead to the breakdown of effective decision-finding processes.

What are the steps in discerning decisions?

The first step in every process of coming to decisions is the recognition that there is something that needs to be decided. There is the recognition of the need for a decision. This may sound banal. Decision-making groups have the responsibility to recognize necessary decisions in a timely manner. If this does not happen, time pressures on the decisions increase, limiting the possibility of proper consideration. The timely recognition of decisions needing to be addressed opens the possibility of forming appropriately inclusive processes. The mandated group identifies the need for a decision, determines who will be impacted by the decision and sets a timeline for the process. They inform the larger group of the need and ask them for any thoughts, questions, or fundamental principles that are pertinent to determining what the decision should be. Those more closely impacted by the decision are invited to a discussion of the issues involved.

The second step lies researching the factors involved in the impending decision, gaining a clear picture of both what is involved and what the possible consequences might be. This stage is followed by a first feedback loop. All those who could be impacted by the decision are given the opportunity to voice their considerations, questions, and thoughts. This feedback gives the group responsible for articulating and socializing the decision a richer picture with which to work. The mandate group weighs the input, decides if the original timeline was correct or if the matter should be studied in more depth. If they determine that they have enough of a sense of the questions to proceed, they move to formulate the possible directions that the decision could take. With these they return to those immediately impacted, then the larger group with the question: We have weighed the input and can see moving in one of these directions. 1) Do you see anything that we have overlooked? 2) Does one of these seem more appropriate than the other?

The third step involves weighing the various aspects involved in the decision and coming to a picture of what might be best for the school at this time. This is a point at which processes often stagnate. The pros and cons for any decision most often balance one another out. Logic has little to do with decisions affecting the lives of people. It is also the point at which principles clash and fundamental questions arise. The group mandated to articulate decisions must navigate its way through these narrows. Clearly guided, structured dialogues, with exercises in picturing, and so forth, are helpful. The second feedback loop comes when the group arrives at what it feels to be a possible decision. Those impacted by this are asked to give their feedback and ask questions.

In a fourth step, the group responsible for the decision reviews the questions and thoughts of those giving feedback and either revises or affirms the decision they had drafted. This is then communicated and affirmed by the appropriate bodies.

By mandating a group to take responsibility for guiding these processes and articulating their outcomes, a school frees other individuals to focus on other aspects of the school's life, most notably the pedagogical questions that lie at the heart of a school's vitality. The smaller mandated group is responsible for discerning what lives in the will of the community and articulating it in such a way that the decision can be lived by those involved. By entrusting this process to a small group, it is possible to transform opposing views rather than compromise the decision by trying to please everyone. Meetings cease to be battlefields where opponents maneuver and strategize in order to achieve their own objectives. They become, instead, a space of engaged listening and dialogue centered on the question: What will we do?

The mandated group is responsible for insuring that those most closely impacted by the decision are given ample opportunity to participate in the process of forming it. If there are clearly opposing points of view, the group must take steps to insure that both sides understand the other's perspective. Understanding plays a key role in finding livable decisions. All trust is rooted in understanding.

Living the Decisions

I remember one school where there were two doors into the reception and administration suite. One day, in a fit of frustration, a mother taped a series of arrows on the floor leading in one door and out the other. On each arrow was printed in bold letters: The buck stops here! This kind of frustration is not uncommon in, though certainly not specific to, Waldorf schools. It echoes Bruno Bettelheim's statement: "Everybody's child is nobody's child." "Everyone's" decision all too often appears to be no one's decision; "everyone's" responsibility, no one's responsibility.

Decisions are never made by groups, only by individuals. Responsibility is never carried by a group, only by an individual. The challenge is not to find decisions that everyone will agree to, but rather to find those that the individuals comprising the group are willing to live together. The "buck" always stops with an individual willing to stand up for the shared intentions of the community, that is: to live these intentions. Living the decisions made in concert with other individuals entails placing my will in service to something higher and more encompassing than my own personal ideas and opinions. In this case, my will serves the decision I now share with my colleagues. Only because each of us has made it, it becomes ours.

Certain situations or challenges in a school community can be addressed only if there is unanimity among those directly affected. Others must be addressed because it has become clear that those directly involved are not able to do so. One school I worked with for a number of years took a good deal of complaint from their umbrella organization for terminating the school's relationship with the entire kindergarten staff and starting over. What was not taken into consideration were the two preceding years when every effort was made to help the kindergarten teachers find a productive working relationship with one another and the school as a whole. The colleagues involved were not able to overcome their personal differences to work together productively as a team. To some extent they had let these differences polarize the parents. Neither colleague was a "bad" teacher. But the dynamic was such that the entire early childhood program was suffering. The initial response to such a situation is to try and do something to fix it. This is an American thing. We try to fix things everywhere. Current events in the Mid-East should have been proof enough about the fallacy of this approach. The challenge isn't to fix things, but to have the courage to engage with them in such a way that change is possible. When the small group of colleagues working with the school's governance team, the group responsible for any decisions regarding personnel, came to the realization that the individuals at the heart of the situation could not take the necessary steps to allow things to change, it became clear that they would have to leave in order to make change possible. Such decisions are never to be taken lightly. It is always better to go the extra yard in helping colleagues make necessary steps. But, on the other hand, there are times when a colleague or, in this case, colleagues must be asked to leave. And one can ask: Who lives such decisions?

A closer look at the way this school has chosen to structure itself can shed some light on this question. Some years ago, the school chose to remove responsibility for making or finding decisions from the faculty as a whole and concentrate this responsibility in smaller mandate groups, which would work in dialogue with the faculty, the Board, and the parent body. This happened in a series of steps that began with a single, four-person governance team responsible for all decisions and progressed to a more decentralized structure with small mandated deciding bodies for the various areas of the school. The governance team remained in place, taking final responsibility for all decisions that affected the school as a whole, including personnel questions, and core groups were formed to be the deciding bodies for early childhood and the lower school, the upper school, and the administrative staff. Each of these core groups took on the responsibility for the day-to-day management of their specific area of focus and, in conjunction with the governance team, provided leadership in articulating and facilitating the exploration of key pedagogical questions pertinent to the future of the school. Faculty meetings took on a consultative role in the decision making/finding process.

Mandating a small group as the deciding body does not relieve the larger circle of responsibility for the decisions. But it does differentiate the question: Who lives this decision? The mandated bodies and those individuals they ask to take an active role in working through a situation or a challenge have to carry the decision. Those who mandated them live the decision by supporting those who have to carry it. The decision to dissolve the kindergartens and start over had to be carried by the governing team and the core group. They delegated a small team to inform the kindergarten colleagues, then, together, they informed first the larger faculty and then the parent body of their decision. Anyone who has been involved in a Waldorf school community can imagine the upheaval that followed. The flames were fanned when one of the kindergarten colleagues, after having first expressed understanding and acceptance of the decision turned to the parents for support. A few parents with strong emotional ties to the teacher took up the call and headed for the barricades. With that wonderful sense of righteousness that flames bright in the battle with injustice, letters were written, emails sent, demands made and meetings called. Governance team and core group members responded to everything with calm understanding, but never wavered. The message they communicated was: "Yes, we understand your grief, and we are aware that this decision has caused you pain. But we are absolutely convinced that this is what is needed."

A number of faculty members not directly involved in the process or the decision had children in kindergarten. They found themselves in a difficult situation. Personally, they found themselves in the position of the other parents; professionally, they had given the deciding bodies their mandate. They spoke openly of this in meetings with the parents and the governance team and, by doing so, were able to raise the question out of the realm of a personal emotional response. Supporting a decision does not mean giving up one's own personal position, but rising above it to a space of shared understanding. One parent finally voiced what would become the community's deep response to what could have been an explosively divisive situation: "At one level, I feel hurt by this decision. My child was happy with K. She has been wonderful with him. On the other hand, we have our children here because we trust that the teachers and staff know what is best for them. If this is what they think is best, I personally am happy to let go of the pain and live with what they have decided."

Space for Initiative

On September 6, 1919, Rudolf Steiner closed the first teacher's course with four principles, which he hoped the teachers would take to heart. The first had to do with intentional engagement. He said: "First, teachers must make sure that they influence and work on their pupils, in a broader sense, by allowing the spirit to flow through their whole being as teachers, and also in the details of their work: how each word is spoken, and how each concept or feeling is developed. Teachers must be people of initiative. They must be filled with initiative. Teachers must never be careless or lazy; they must, at every moment, stand in full consciousness of what they do in the school and how they act toward the children. This is the first principle. The teacher must be a person of initiative in everything done, great and small."[60]

What Steiner says here about the relationship between teacher and child holds true for the entire school as a social organism. "This is the first principle. The teacher must be a person of initiative in everything done, great and small." Individual initiative is the life-blood of a school community.

It begins with small things. Pieces of paper on the ground, words of care for an unhappy child, a helping hand for a stressed colleague, flowers for a faculty meeting. Initiative begins as the courage to live as though your life could make a difference. It is often easier in the heady days of a young school or endeavor and more difficult as the school ages, people become more set in their ways and institutional forms become stronger. Initiative in the social realm always has a quality of spontaneity or youthfulness. It reaches across the protective boundaries of routine and convention, ignores the abstract categories created by positions and acquired roles and connects one individual directly to another. Individual initiative is the only thing that can overcome the soporific effect of institutional structures with their rules and regulations, their policies and procedures. As one colleague said after a year of working with a new organizational structure with clearly articulated roles and functions, a superb committee structure with mapped out chains of communication, forms to fill out, details of who reports to whom when, who is reviewed by whom in which rhythm, and so forth: "Everything runs well, but it is impossible to try anything new. It doesn't nurture change or cultivate initiative."

As the Waldorf school movement moves ever farther away from its roots, the question of initiative becomes more important. There are two sides to this question. One has to do with the identity of Waldorf education — its spiritual integrity — and the other with the changing face of childhood. The forms adopted in 1919 to make a Waldorf school possible in post-war southern Germany certainly no longer speak to the developmental reality of children growing up in America today. And even then, Steiner spoke explicitly about the inadequacy of the forms. In his first lecture to prospective parents in Stuttgart 1919, he said: "We will, therefore, be unable to organize our educational material so that it represents what we find to be the ideal of a truly humane education. In a manner of speaking, we will be able to use only the holes that still remain in the tightly woven web that spreads over the educational system. In these holes we will work to instruct the children entrusted to the Waldorf School in the sense of a completely free cultural life. We plan to take full advantage of every opportunity presented. We most certainly will not be able to create a model school."[61]

The challenge of creatively using the "holes in the tightly woven web" has been taken up by teachers in various schools around the world in a refreshing variety of ways. Marisha Plotnik described the emergence of the open, collaborative Math Lab at the Rudolf Steiner School in Manhattan:

Nearly a decade ago, a change in the music program left high school students with a free period in the week. When this schedule was presented to the faculty, this time was framed as "appointment hour." This was described as, and indeed became, an opportunity for students to meet individually with their teachers, nearly all of whom were free during that period. This became a natural time for students to seek extra help in math. Perhaps because some of the math teachers also teach music, students began to meet not only with their own particular math teacher, but with any available member of the math department. As the number of students increased, the mood of these meetings changed from individual tutoring to a cooperative learning endeavor, and Math Lab was born. During the last three years, Math Lab has expanded, and it now also takes place three days a week after school and includes students in grades six, seven, and eight.

Math Lab is a time when anything can happen. Perhaps no one shows up. Perhaps the room is crowded with seventh graders vociferously arguing about what just happened in the stairwell. Or perhaps three sixth-grade girls are standing at the chalkboard working together on a problem about lights in a hallway that points towards a unique quality of the perfect squares (although they do not know that yet). One seventh grader shows up every week because it is a nice quiet place to work on homework. One tenth grader reluctantly dragged herself there on Tuesday and did her best ten minutes of math work for the entire week. Although certain students are urged to attend every week, the not-quite-compulsory nature of attendance—and the fact that anyone is welcome to drop in at any time—changes the dynamics of the group every time.

Thus Math Lab has become a space for initiative. It is an attempt to de-institutionalize the learning of math within the institution of school. We work together to make sense of mathematics in the way that seems most responsive to the moment. We come with our own questions, thoughts, and ideas, any one of which may be left at the door or may become the leading thought of the day. It has become my favorite teaching time in the week.

There is a decidedly conservative tendency in education. This is also true in the Waldorf school movement. Until recently, there was strong inclination to view the Stuttgart school as the model Steiner explicitly said it would not be able to be— except in as much as it was able to identify and work creatively with the holes remaining "in the tightly woven web that spreads over the educational system." Although this has changed somewhat in recent years, we are still more likely to embrace what has been done before than venture into the uncertainty of what has not yet been tried.

In terms of school governance, the question we face is: Can we govern ourselves in such a way that we have the courage to support one another as we face the educational challenges coming to meet us? Do our governance forms support the taking of pedagogical initiative? Does school culture nurture the deepening of anthroposophical understanding? In a recent conversation concerning the role of faculty study one colleague commented: "The more I work with Steiner's pedagogical lectures, the less I rely on the 'curriculum' to tell me what I'm supposed to be doing."

The Evolving Social Organism

In 1989, Frank Teichmann published an essay titled "The Evolution of Evolution."[62] It is an intriguing piece that follows the development of the idea of evolution in the work of Goethe and his contemporaries. He shows how two things coincide: Goethe's awakening sense of his own capacity for inner growth and his capacity to recognize the natural artistry of change in the world around him. Teichmann writes: "Goethe's observation is of the utmost significance for the emergence of the idea of evolution. The idea of evolution cannot be seen or found in the environment if the fact of evolution is not first experienced within a human being. A person who is not himself in the process of evolving will not be able to recognize evolution." The source of individual evolution lies within the individual: "Nature makes of man merely a natural being; society makes of him a law-abiding being; only he can make of himself a free being. Nature releases man from her fetters at a certain stage of his development; society carries this development a stage further; he alone can give himself the final polish."[63]

The evolutionary source of individual growth lies within the individual human being. What is the source of evolution in a social organism? There is no simple answer to this question. Teichmann calls our attention to one aspect. In summarizing the early efforts of the German idealists to conceptualize evolution, he writes: "They recognize evolution as occurring between the activity of a spiritual being — which always remains identical with itself — and its changing manifestations over time. Whenever we use the term evolution we should keep in mind that we are speaking of a being. We may focus on a sense perceptible manifestation, but this does not mean the being does not exist, only that we, for the moment, have forgotten it."

With this in mind, the question concerning the source of evolution of a school — a social organism — can be re-framed: Which being brings itself to expression in the school's biography? And: How can we come to know and work productively with this being?

Thus, at the end of these explorations, we arrive at the question that has been present in some form from the beginning. There is something elusive about this question. I sit here with my pen poised above the paper; I can see in my mind's eye the presence of this being in various schools with which I been involved; I remember moments when its presence was palpable in the room. But it is very difficult to find the words that can express it properly. One experiences the being, the spirit, the commanding presence of a school in much the same way one experiences beauty or truth or goodness. One experiences it as an active presence. It is most tangible in moments when a circle of colleagues[64] are able to rise above their own personal considerations and step into a space of intentional receptivity around questions concerning the future of the school. In such moments, it is possible for something higher, an experienced presence to express itself through the individual members of the circle. There is a similarity between this experience and what the three members of Shackleton's expedition experienced on their final trek across South Georgia Island. Such moments have a quality of sublime grace; each one present feels raised above personal limitations: everyone recognizes that something new is possible.

It is my personal conviction that self-governance can only be successful if it is centered on the striving to make such moments of communion possible.

Notes

1. Steiner, Rudolf. *Faculty Meetings with Rudolf Steiner.* 2 vols. 1919-1922 and 1922-1924. Hudson, NY: Anthroposophic Press, 1998

2. Steiner, Rudolf. "The Threefold Social Order and Educational Freedom" in *The Renewal of the Social Organism.* Hudson NY: Anthroposophic Press, 1985

3. Steiner, Rudolf. *The Foundations of Human Experience.* Hudson NY: Anthroposophic Press, 1996

4. Steiner, Rudolf. *Study of Man.* London: Rudolf Steiner Press, 1966

5. Steiner, Rudolf. *The Child's Changing Consciousness.* Hudson, NY: Anthroposophic Press, 1996

6. I am deeply indebted to Adam Hochschild for his telling of the story of the *Zong* in *Bury the Chains.* Boston and New York.: Houghton Mifflin Company, 2005

7. Hochschild, p. 80

8. Hochschild, p. 80

9. Hochschild, p. 88

10. Hochschild, p. 88

11. Hochschild, p. 89

12. Emerson, Ralph Waldo. *Emerson's Essays: First & Second Series Complete in One Volume.* New York: Thomas Y. Crowell, 1981

13. The German term used here is *Geistesleben.* The literal translation ("spiritual life") is somewhat misleading. In German the term refers to the thinking life of a culture, universities are centers of a culture *Geistesleben*, as well as churches. In English, the term is used in a narrower sense; it is, however, less clearly defined as in German.

14. Steiner, Rudolf. *The Foundations of Human Experience.* Hudson NY: Anthroposophic Press, 1996

15. Steiner, Rudolf. *The Renewal of the Social Organism.* Hudson NY: Anthroposophic Press, 1985

16. Lindenberg, Christoph. *Rudolf Steiner: A Biography.* Great Barrington, MA: SteinerBooks, 2012

17. Steiner, Rudolf. *The Foundations of Human Experience.* Hudson NY: Anthroposophic Press, 1996

18. Steiner, Rudolf. *Rudolf Steiner in the Waldorf School.* Hudson NY: Anthroposophic Press, 1996

19. Only after WWII as the number of Waldorf schools began to increase evermore rapidly did the practices begin to be codified.

20. Quotations throughout this chapter have been taken from the transcripts of Rudolf Steiner's meetings with the faculty of the first Waldorf School. The transcripts have been published in English under the title: *Faculty Meetings With Rudolf Steiner.* 2 vols. 1919-1922 and 1922-1924. Hudson NY: Anthroposophic Press, 1998

21. Although we often speak about Rudolf Steiner's social impulse, it is rarely reflected in the structures and practices common in Waldorf schools and other anthroposophical institutions.

22. Chadha, Yogesh. *Gandhi, A Life.* New York: John Wiley & Sons, 1997

23. Steiner, Rudolf. *Balance in Teaching.* Great Barrington MA: SteinerBooks, 2007

24. Fischer, Louis. *The Life of Mahatma Gandhi.* New York NY: Collier Books, 1973

25. Fischer, p. 49

26. Fischer, p. 122

27. Quoted in Fischer, p. 124

28. Steiner, Rudolf. *The Philosophy of Freedom.* London: Rudolf Steiner Press, 1979

29. The Center for Contextual Studies is a decentralized research community founded to engage in and support collaborative action-based research that can lead beyond the current boundaries of conventional knowledge to a quality of understanding that enables

human consciousness to participate fully in the spiritual reality of our world and the forces shaping it.

30. The Partnership for 21st Century Skills was formed to serve as a catalyst to position 21st century readiness at the center of US K-12 education by building collaborative partnerships among education, business, community and government leaders. It was founded in 2002 by a coalition of large corporations including both Microsoft and Apple working in collaboration with the US Department of Education.

31. Shaping School Culture: Excerpts from an interview with Dr. Kent Peterson. Apple Learning Exchange http://ali.apple.com/ ali_sites/ali/exhibits/1000488/

32. Peterson, Shaping School Culture

33. Steiner, Rudolf. *Autobiography*. Great Barrington MA: Steiner-Books, 2006

34. Steiner, *Autobiography*, p. 163

35. Steiner, *Autobiography*, p. 164

36. Steiner, *Autobiography*, p. 165

37. Steiner, Rudolf. *The Education of the Child and Early Lectures Education*. Hudson NY: Anthroposophic Press, 1996

38. Saint Augustine. *Confessions*. Baltimore MD: Penguin Books, 1966

39. Steiner, Rudolf. Lecture from October 10, 1916 in Zurich, Switzerland

40. Steiner, Rudolf. *The Foundations of Human Experience*. Hudson NY: Anthroposophic Press, 1996

41. Robert K. Greenleaf (1904-1990) was founder of the Servant leadership movement and Greenleaf Center for Servant Leadership. In 1970 he published his first essay, entitled "The Servant as Leader," which introduced the term "servant leadership." Later, the essay was expanded into a book, which is perhaps one of the most influential management texts yet written: *Servant Leadership* (1977; 25th anniversary edition, Mahwah NJ: Paulist Press, 2002), now subtitled *A Journey into the Nature of Legitimate Power & Greatness*. Though his terms are secular, his definition of leadership is the clearest statement of his belief that the needs of followers are holy and legitimate, and the leaders use of power arises from the consent of the followers.

42. DePree, Max. *Leadership Is an Art.* New York: Dell Publishing 1990

43. Shackleton, Ernest. *South.* New York NY: Carroll & Graf Publishers, 1998

44. Shackleton, p. 77

45. Shackleton, p. 121

46. Shackleton, p. 207

47. Shackleton, p. 211

48. Steiner, Rudolf. *How to Know Higher Worlds.* Great Barrington MA: Anthroposophic Press, 1994

49. I am embarrassed to say that I can no longer find the source of this quote. I had jotted it down on a piece of paper in a folder dedicated to the Threefold Campaign in Stuttgart in 1919–20, but neglected to note the source.

50. Covey, Stephen R. *The 7 Habits of Highly Effective People.* New York NY: Simon and Schuster, Inc., 1989

51. Covey, p. 101

52. I have been asked a number of times if these two bodies are the Board and the College. Yes, and no. In the organizational structure most common in American Waldorf schools, the Board is legally responsible for the existence of the school as a corporate body. The idea of the "College" suffers from a lack of clarity about its role, its function and its spiritual basis. In an ideal situation, one could imagine Board and College taking on these two polar functions. In contemporary practice, there is much confusion concerning which "body" is responsible for what. In the confusion, Colleges at times function as spiritually correct "overBoards," and Boards find themselves stepping in to ensure the continuance of Waldorf education.

53. Hahn, Herbert. *Der Weg der mich fuehrte.* Stuttgart, Germany: Freies Geistesleben, 1969

54. Glasl, F, and Lievegoed, B. *Dynamische Unternehmensentwicklung.* Bern, CH: Paul Haupt, 1993

55. Steiner, Rudolf. *Towards Social Renewal.* London: Rudolf Steiner Press, 1999

56. Steiner, *Towards Social Renewal.* 1999

57. Suchantke, Andreas. *Metamorphosis*. Hillsdale NY: Adonis Press, 2009

58. Wember, Valentin. *Wille zur Verantwortung*. Stuttgart, Germany: Stratos Verlag, 2012 (translation by author)

59. Rilke, Rainer Maria. *Letters to a Young Poet*. Boston MA: Shambahala, 1993

60. Steiner, Rudolf. *Discussions with Teachers*. Hudson NY: Anthroposophic Press, 1997

61. Steiner, Rudolf. *The Spirit of the Waldorf School*. Hudson NY: Anthroposophic Press, 1995

62. Teichmann, Frank. "The Evolution of Evolution" first printed in *Interdisciplinary Aspects of Evolution*. Stuttgart, Germany: Urachhaus, 1989

63. Steiner, Rudolf. *The Philosophy of Freedom*. London: Rudolf Steiner Press, 1979

64. I use the term colleagues here in a descriptive, not a formal manner. It describes a quality of activity. A colleague is anyone in a school who is willing to engage in this quality of activity. Teachers, parents, administrative staff, groundskeepers, and Board members are all potential colleagues.

About the Author

Jon McAlice began teaching in 1976 at East Hill Farm School in southern Vermont. He brought to this work skills in boatbuilding and carpentry and a love of explorative inquiry that stood him in good stead for his work with adolescents in the classroom, the workshop, and on the school's organic farm. During this time, he was involved in various forms of social activism, especially with the Catholic Worker Movement and the Movement for a New Community, working with the homeless and with street children on Manhattan's Lower East Side. The death of a close friend living at the Camphill community in Copake, NY, brought him to a decisive encounter with the work of Rudolf Steiner. He left America in 1984 and moved to Dornach, Switzerland, to study at the Rudolf Steiner Lehrerseminar. He earned his Waldorf teaching diploma there, studying at night, while also heading up the woodworking shop at the Goetheanum. In 1989, he joined Heinz Zimmermann in the Educational Section of the Goetheanum and spent the next 11 years working for the international Waldorf school movement. His primary responsibilities included the international aspects of the Section's work and coordinating research projects on topics such as curriculum development, school governance, and the relation between school culture and the evolving nature of work. During this period he founded and edited the *Educational Section Journal,* a bilingual journal for Waldorf educators; co-founded and became one of the first executive co-directors of the International Association for Waldorf Education East, supporting the growth of the Waldorf school movements in the Eastern European countries; and worked closely with the Freunde der Erziehungskunst to further the growth of Waldorf education in developing countries. Meanwhile he continued to teach, organize conferences, lecture, and conduct workshops. In 2000, he returned to the U.S., initially to the Bay area. From 2001 to 2004, he was the high school coordinator for Summerfield Waldorf School, responsible for teacher and program development. He also initiated and led regional high school teachers' workshops and initiated and co-led Young Teachers conferences and the Advanced Studies Initiative. In 2008, Jon co-founded the Center for Contextual Studies, a decentralized research collaborative formed to engage in and support collaborative action-based research that can lead beyond the current boundaries of conventional knowledge to a quality of understanding that enables human consciousness to participate fully in the spiritual reality of our world and the forces shaping it. In 2006, he and his family returned to the Northeast, settling in Ghent, N.Y., where he continues his work as a designer, researcher, teacher, and consultant.